# The World's Favourite Love Poems

# The World's Favourite Love Poems

Compiled and Introduced by
Suheil Bushrui

ONEWORLD

A Oneworld Book

Published by Oneworld Publications 2008
Copyright © Suheil Bushrui 2008
Reprinted 2008
This edition published in 2013

ISBN 978–1–85168–982-8
ebook ISBN 978–1–78074-069-0

Typeset by Jayvee, Trivandrum, India
Cover design by James Nunn
Printed and bound by TJ International, Cornwall, UK

Oneworld Publications
10 Bloomsbury Street
London WC1B 3SR
England
www.oneworld-publications.com

Stay up to date with the latest books,
special offers, and exclusive content from
Oneworld with our monthly newsletter

Sign up on our website
**www.oneworld-publications.com**

*Dedicated to Bechara and Rita Nammour*
*In honour of the 30th anniversary of their marriage*
*March 30, 2008*
*and*
*in admiration of the unique relationship*
*of love and loyalty for each other that shines*
*like a ray of light and inspires all those who are*
*entering the realm of sacred matrimony*

\*

No relationship between two people is genuine or true
until each to the other speaks as 'I' instead of 'you'.

*From the Arabic*

# CONTENTS

# INTRODUCTION

THE PROFOUND universal experience of love is impossible to define; it can be known only by its manifestations, both secular and divine. Whatever may be the vicissitudes of love, Tennyson may be right when he categorically states:

> I hold it true, whate'er befall,
> I feel it, when I sorrow most,
> 'Tis better to have loved and lost
> Than never to have loved at all.

The creative power of love reveals itself most eloquently in poetic form, for without poetry love is wordless, and without love poetry lacks an energy and dynamism that only love can generate. In the following selections of love poetry borrowed from the diverse cultural traditions of the world, complete poems and extracts from longer works are included. The poems selected are by recognized masters as well as lesser poets—all of whom have inspired successive generations of men and women everywhere.

* * *

In a famous passage [translated by Sir Richard Livingstone], the Greek playwright Sophocles equates love with Aphrodite, suggesting the complex and contradictory elements of what we call love:

> But in her name lie many names concealed:
> for she is Death, imperishable Force.
> Desire unmixed, wild Frenzy, Lamentation:
> in her are summed all impulses that drive
> to Violence, Energy, Tranquillity.
> Deep in each living breast the Goddess sinks,
> and all become her prey; the tribes that swim,
> the fourfoot tribes that pace upon the earth,
> harbour her; and in birds her wing is sovereign.
> In beasts, in mortal men, in gods above.
> What god but wrestles with her and is thrown?
> If I may tell—and truth is right to tell—
> she rules the heart of Zeus without a spear,
> without a sword. Truly the Cyprian
> shatters all purposes of men and gods.

With obvious difficulty Sophocles is trying to define the indefinable, and in this passage both the negative and the positive aspects of love are mentioned. The attitudes, the vicissitudes, and the caprices of love have led many a philosopher, thinker, and poet to come up with as many definitions as there are lovers. For love is sometimes described as 'madness' and 'the wildest woe'. At other times, it is 'the salt of life' and 'the sweetest joy'. Whether it is this or that or a combination of both, no one who has truly loved can deny the healing power, the creative energy, the exhilaration, the glory, the majesty, and the awe-inspiring magnificence that love engenders in the heart. Some believe that love does not last; others hold fast to their faith in the enduring power of love. In Christian terms, 'God is love', while the Sufi poet cried out that only God 'knows what manner of love is mine'. What remains true, however, is that unique experience which reaches its complete fulfilment in a love that is truly sublime:

> It is that love which reaches out to you even when you
> do not ask for it.
> It is bestowed upon you even when you do not deserve
> it.
> It renews the spirit and uplifts the heart.
> It teaches humility and reveals compassion.
> It was there yesterday, it is here today, and it will most
> certainly be there tomorrow.

* * *

Notwithstanding the difficulties that face the editor of any selection of love poetry, the more acute problem here was to decide on the languages to be represented. In this respect, I sought the help of *The New Princeton Encyclopedia of Poetry and Prosody* which divided love poetry into two main categories: the love poetry of the Western world and the love poetry of the Eastern world. The first category was general and did not specify any number of languages; the second, that of the Eastern world, the Encyclopedia divided into seven language groups: Ancient Egyptian, Arabic, Chinese, Hebrew, Indian, Japanese, and Persian.

In this collection, I have adopted this system as far as the Eastern world is concerned, but I added to the seven language groups that have been mentioned other poems from Africa and Australasia, as well as poems taken from the love poetry of the first people. I divided the Western world into eight language groups: Ancient Greek and Latin, English, French, German, Italian, Portuguese, Spanish, and Russian.

Any selection made leaves its editor with a sense of profound dissatisfaction with his work, for it is very easy to say: 'If this were added, it would be better, while if this were omitted, it would redeem some weakness.' No selection whatsoever can be perfect or complete.

Perhaps the following immortal lines from Shakespeare set a universal standard for what true love could be:

> Let me not to the marriage of true minds
> Admit impediments. Love is not love
> Which alters when it alteration finds,
> Or bends with the remover to remove:
> O no! It is an ever-fixed mark
> That looks on tempests and is never shaken;
> It is the star to every wand'ring bark,
> Whose worth's unknown, although his height be taken.
> Love's not Time's fool, though rosy lips and cheeks
> Within his bending sickle's compass come;
> Love alters not with his brief hours and weeks,
> But bears it out even to the edge of doom.
> If this be error and upon me proved,
> I never writ, nor no man ever loved.

# ON LOVE ITSELF

## Kathleen Raine

Amo Ergo Sum

Because I love
    The sun pours out its rays of living gold
    Pours out its gold and silver on the sea.

Because I love
    The earth upon her astral spindle winds
    Her ecstasy-producing dance.

Because I love
    Clouds travel on the winds through wide skies,
    Skies wide and beautiful, blue and deep.

Because I love
    Wind blows white sails,
    The wind blows over flowers, the sweet wind blows.

Because I love
    The ferns grow green, and green the grass, and green
    The transparent sunlit trees.

Because I love
    Larks rise up from the grass
    And all the leaves are full of singing birds.

Because I love
    The summer air quivers with a thousand wings,
    Myriads of jewelled eyes burn in the light.

Because I love
    The iridescent shells upon the sand
    Takes forms as fine and intricate as thought.

Because I love
    There is an invisible way across the sky,
    Birds travel by that way, the sun and moon
    And all the stars travel that path by night.

Because I love
    There is a river flowing all night long.

Because I love
    All night the river flows into my sleep,
    Ten thousand living things are sleeping in my arms,
    And sleeping wake, and flowing are at rest.

# Strato

Love's Immortality

Who may know if a loved one passes the prime, while ever with him and never left alone? Who may not satisfy to-day who satisfied yesterday? And if he satisfy, what should befall him not to satisfy to-morrow?

—translated from the Greek by John William Mackail

## Percy Bysshe Shelley

*from* Epipsychidion

True Love in this differs from gold and clay,
That to divide is not to take away.
Love is like understanding, that grows bright,
Gazing on many truths; 'tis like thy light,
Imagination! which from earth and sky,
And from the depths of human phantasy,
As from a thousand prisms and mirrors, fills
The Universe with glorious beams, and kills
Error, the worm, with many a sun-like arrow
Of its reverberated lightning. Narrow
The heart that loves, the brain that contemplates,
The life that wears,
the spirit that creates
One object, and one form, and builds thereby
A sepulchre for its eternity.

# Jámí

## Layla and Majnun

When the Dawn of Eternity whispered of Love, Love cast the Fire
of Longing into the Pen.

The Pen raised its head from the Tablet of Not-Being, and drew a
hundred pictures of wondrous aspect.

The Heavens are the offspring of Love: the Elements fell to Earth
through Love.

Without Love is no token of Good or Evil: that thing which is not of
Love is indeed non-existent.

This lofty azure Roof which revolveth through the days and nights

Is the Lotus of the Garden of Love, and all the Ball [which lies] in
the curve of Love's Polo-stick.

That Magnetism which is inherent in the Stone, and which fastens
its grasp so firmly on the Iron,

Is a Love precipitated in Iron Resolve which hath appeared from
within the Stone.

Behold the Stone, how in this resting-place it becomes without
weight through longing for its opponent:

Judge therefrom of those who suffer sorrow in the attraction of the
love of those dear to the heart.

Although Love is painful, it is the consolation of pure bosoms.

Without the blessing of Love how shall a man escape from the
sorrow of the inverted Wheel [of Heaven]?

*—translated from the Persian by Edward G. Browne*

# e. e. cummings

love is a place


love is a place
& through this place of
love move
(with brightness of peace)
all places

yes is a world
& in this world of
yes live
(skilfully curled)
all worlds

# Juan Ramón Jiménez

## Were I Reborn


Were I reborn a stone,
even so I should love you, woman.

Were I reborn as wind,
even so I should love you, woman.

Were I reborn a wave,
even so I should love you, woman.

Were I reborn as fire,
even so I should love you, woman.

Were I reborn a man,
even so I should love you, woman.

*—translated from the Spanish by Eleanor L. Turnbull*

# John Donne

## A Lecture Upon the Shadow

Stand still, and I will read to thee
A lecture, Love, in Love's philosophy.
   These three hours that we have spent,
   Walking here, two shadows went
Along with us, which we ourselves produced.
But, now the sun is just above our head,
   We do those shadows tread,
   And to brave clearness all things are reduced.
So whilst our infant loves did grow,
Disguises did, and shadows, flow
From us and our cares; but now 'tis not so.

That love hath not attain'd the highest degree,
Which is still diligent lest others see.

Except our loves at this noon stay,
We shall new shadows make the other way.
   As the first were made to blind
   Others, these which come behind
Will work upon ourselves, and blind our eyes.
If our loves faint, and westwardly decline,
   To me thou, falsely, thine
   And I to thee mine actions shall disguise.
The morning shadows wear away,
But these grow longer all the day;
But O! love's day is short, if love decay.

Love is a growing, or full constant light,
And his short minute, after noon, is night.

# Anonymous

We only know the one we love
Not the one who loves us.
Love is of many kinds.
One love says: if you die let me die with you.
Another love says: if you buy the stew, I will buy the rice.
There is love of the eye,
There is love of the mouth.
The love of the wife is different,
The love of the husband is different,
The love of the father is different,
The love of the mother is greatest.
It is love that makes the goat share her husband's beard.
'I see the one I want to marry.'
The father says: 'Don't you know that his father is deaf?'
'If the whip howls on my back, and thunder shouts in heaven,
    If you tie me to the pillar and feed me with grass like a horse,
    I will still know whom I love!'

*—translated from the Yoruba by Robert Cameron Mitchell*

# Coventry Patmore

## The Revelation

An idle poet, here and there,
    Looks round him, but, for all the rest,
The world, unfathomably fair,
    Is duller than a witling's jest.
Love wakes men, once a lifetime each;
    They lift their heavy lids, and look;
And, lo, what one sweet page can teach,
    They read with joy, then shut the book.
And give some thanks, and some blaspheme,
    And most forget, but, either way,
That and the child's unheeded dream
    Is all the light of all their day.

# Li Bai

## The Melody at a Spring Night

Hearing the sound of a flute, on a spring night in Luo Cheng,
[I wonder] from whose jade flute this melody is flying secretly in the
    dark?
Vibrating and scattering around, merging gently in the spring breeze,
it fills the air and the heaven of Luo Cheng;
On such a night, I hear in the middle of its singing music
the bending and dancing of the trembling willow.
Whose heart would not be moved by sentiments and love,
soaring with the thoughts of precious home?

*—translated from the Chinese by Ninaz Shadman*

9

# Percy Bysshe Shelley

## Love's Philosophy

The Fountains mingle with the river
And the rivers with the ocean,
The winds of heaven mix for ever
With a sweet emotion;
Nothing in the world is single,
All things by a law devine
In one another's being mingle—
Why not I with thine?

See the mountains kiss high heaven
And the waves clasp one another;
No sister-flower would be forgiven
If it disdain'd its brother:
And the sunlight clasps the earth,
And the moonbeams kiss the sea—
What are all these kissings worth,
If thou kiss not me?

# William Blake

## Injunction

The Angel that presided o'er my birth
Said, 'Little creature, formed of joy and mirth
Go love, without the help of any thing on earth.'

# Jalálu'ddín Rúmí

*from* The House of Love

This house wherein is continually the sound of the viol,
Ask of the Master, what house is this?
If it is the Ka'ba, what means this idol-form?
And if it is the Magian temple, what means this light of God?
In this house is a treasure which the universe is too small to hold;
This 'house' and this 'Master' is all acting and pretence.
Lay no hand on the house, for this house is a talisman;
Speak not with the Master, for he is drunken overnight.
The dust and rubbish of this house is all musk and perfume,
The roof and door of this house is all verse and melody.
In fine, whoever has found his way into this house
Is the sultan of the world and the Solomon of the time.
O Master, bend down thy head once from this roof,
For in thy fair face is a token of fortune.
Like a mirror, the Soul has received thy image in its heart;
The tip of thy curl has sunk into its heart like a comb.
This is the Lord of Heaven, who resembles Venus and the moon;
This is the House of Love, which hath no bound or end.

*—translated from the Persian by Reynold A. Nicholson*

# Andrew Marvell

## The Definition of Love

My Love is of a birth as rare
    As 'tis, for object, strange and high;
It was begotten by Despair,
    Upon Impossibility.

Magnanimous Despair alone
    Could show me so divine a thing,
Where feeble hope could ne'er have flown,
    But vainly flapped its tinsel wing.

And yet I quickly might arrive
    Where my extended soul is fixed;
But Fate does iron wedges drive,
    And always crowds itself betwixt.

For Fate with jealous eye does see
    Two perfect loves, nor lets them close;
Their union would her ruin be,
    And her tyrannic power depose.

And therefore her decrees of steel
    Us as the distant poles have placed,
(Though Love's whole world on us doth wheel),
    Not by themselves to be embraced,

Unless the giddy heaven fall,
    And earth some new convulsion tear.
And, us to join, the world should all
    Be cramp'd into a planisphere.

As lines, so love's oblique, may well
   Themselves in every angle greet:
But ours, so truly parallel,
   Though infinite, can never meet.

Therefore the love which us doth bind,
   But Fate so enviously debars,
Is the conjunction of the mind,
   And opposition of the stars.

# Ovid

*from* The Heroic Epistle


A spring there is whose silver waters show,
Clear as a glass, the shining sands below:
A flowery lotus spreads its arms above,
Shades all the banks and seems itself a grove;
Eternal greens the mossy margin grace,
Watched by the sylvan genius of the place:
Here as I lay, and swelled with tears the flood
Before my sight a watery virgin stood:
She stood and cried, 'O you that love in vain,
Fly hence and seek the fair Leucadian main:
There stands a rock from whose impending steep
Apollo's fane surveys the rolling deep;
There injured lovers, leaping from above,
Their flames extinguish and forget to love.
Deucalion once with hopeless fury burned;
In vain he loved, relentless Pyrrha scorned.
But when from hence he plunged into the main,
Deucalion scorned, and Pyrrha loved in vain.
Haste, Sappho, haste, from high Leucadia throw
Thy wretched weight, nor dread the deeps below.'
She spoke, and vanished with the voice: I rise,
And silent tears fall trickling from my eyes.
I go, ye nymphs, those rocks and seas to prove:
How much I fear, but ah, how much I love!
I go, ye nymphs, where furious love inspires;
Let female fears submit to female fires:
To rocks and seas I fly from Phaon's hate,
And hope from seas and rocks a milder fate.
Ye gentle gales, beneath my body blow,
And softly lay me on the waves below.

And thou, kind Love, my sinking limbs sustain,
Spread thy soft wings and waft me o'er the main,
Nor let a lover's death the guiltless flood profane.
On Phoebus' shrine my harp I'll then bestow,
And this inscription shall be placed below:—
'Here she who sung, to him that did inspire,
Sappho to Phoebus consecrates her lyre:
What suits with Sappho, Phoebus, suits with thee;
The gift, the giver, and the god agree.'

*—translated from the Latin by Alexander Pope*

# Robert Burns

## A Red, Red Rose

O my luve's like a red, red rose
That's newly sprung in June;
O my luve's like the melodie
That's sweetly play'd in tune.

As fair art thou, my bonnie lass,
So deep in luve am I;
And I will luve thee still, my dear,
Till a' the seas gang dry.

Till a' the seas gang dry, my dear,
And the rocks melt wi' the sun;
O I will luve thee still, my dear
While the sands o' life shall run.

And fare-thee-weel, my only Luve!
And fare-thee-weel awhile!
And I will come again, my Luve,
Tho' 'twere ten thousand miles.

O my luve's like a red, red rose,
That's newly sprung in June;
O my luve's like the melodie
That's sweetly play'd in tune.

# Kabir

Hang up the swing of love today!
Hang the body and the mind between the
  arms of the beloved, in the ecstasy of love's joy:
Bring the tearful streams of the rainy clouds
  to your eyes, and cover your heart with
  the shadow of darkness:
Bring your face nearer to his ear, and speak
  of the deepest longings of your heart.
Kabir says: 'Listen to me brother! Bring the
  vision of the Beloved in your heart.'

*—translated from Bengali by Rabindranath Tagore*

# William Blake

The Clod and the Pebble

'Love seeketh not itself to please,
Nor for itself hath any care;
But for another gives its ease,
And builds a Heaven in Hell's despair.'

So sang a little Clod of Clay,
Trodden with the cattle's feet;
But a Pebble of the brook,
Warbled out these metres meet:

'Love seeketh only Self to please,
To bind another to its delight;
Joys in another's loss of ease,
And builds a Hell in Heaven's despite.'

# Johann Wolfgang von Goethe

*from* The West-Eastern Divan

Book of books most wonderful
Is sure the book of Love;
Heedfully I have read it through;
Of joys some scanty leaves,
Whole sheets writ o'er with pain;
Separation forms a section,
Reunion a little chapter,
And that a fragment. Troubles run to volumes,
Drawn out with due elucidations,
Endless and measureless.
O Nisami!—yet at last
It was the right way thou didst find;
The insoluble, ah! who can solve it?
Lovers, when heart once more meets heart.

*—translated from the German by Edward Dowden*

# Elizabeth Barrett Browning

*from* Sonnets from the Portuguese

How do I love thee? Let me count the ways.
I love thee to the depth and breadth and height
My soul can reach, when feeling out of sight
For the ends of Being and ideal Grace.
I love thee to the level of everyday's
Most quiet need, by sun and candle light.
I love thee freely, as men strive for Right;
I love thee purely, as they turn from Praise.
I love thee with the passion put to use
In my old griefs, and with my childhood's faith.
I love thee with a love I seemed to lose
With my lost saints—I love thee with the breath,
Smiles, tears, of all my life!—and, if God choose,
I shall but love thee better after death.

# Omar Khayyam

*from* The Rubaiyat


## 11

Here with a Loaf of Bread beneath the Bough,
A Flask of Wine, a Book of Verse—and Thou
Beside me singing in the Wilderness—
And Wilderness is Paradise enow.


## 20

Ah! my Beloved, fill the Cup that clears
TO-DAY of past Regrets and future Fears—
To-morrow?—Why, To-morrow I may be
Myself with Yesterday's Sev'n Thousand Years.


## 21

Lo! some we loved, the loveliest and best
That Time and Fate of all their Vintage prest,
Have drunk their Cup a Round or two before,
And one by one crept silently to Rest.


## 23

Ah, make the most of what we yet may spend,
Before we too into the Dust descend;
Dust into Dust, and under Dust, to lie,
Sans Wine, sans Song, sans Singer, and—sans End!

Oh, come with old Khayyám, and leave the Wise
To talk; one thing is certain, that Life flies;
One thing is certain, and the Rest is Lies;
The Flower that once has blown for ever dies.


32


There was a Door to which I found no Key:
There was a Veil past which I could not see:
Some little Talk awhile of ME and THEE;
There seemed—and then no more of THEE and ME.


56


And this I know: whether the one True Light,
Kindle to Love, or Wrath consume me quite,
One Glimpse of It within the Tavern caught
Better than in the Temple lost outright.


73


Ah Love! could thou and I with Fate conspire
To grasp this sorry Scheme of Things entire,
Would not we shatter it to bits—and then
Re-mould it nearer to the Heart's Desire!

*—translated from the Persian by Edward Fitzgerald*

# Ralph Waldo Emerson

*from* Give All to Love

Give all to love;
Obey thy heart;
Friends, kindred, days,
Estate, good fame,
Plans, credit, and the muse;
Nothing refuse.

'Tis a brave master,
Let it have scope,
Follow it utterly,
Hope beyond hope;
High and more high,
It dives into noon,
With wing unspent,
Untold intent;
But 'tis a god,
Knows its own path,
And the outlets of the sky.
'Tis not for the mean,
It requireth courage stout,
Souls above doubt,
Valor unbending;
Such 'twill reward,
They shall return
More than they were,
And ever ascending.

Leave all for love;—
Yet, hear me, yet,
One word more thy heart behoved,

One pulse more of firm endeavor,
Keep thee to-day,
To-morrow, for ever,
Free as an Arab
Of thy beloved.
Cling with life to the maid;
But when the surprise,
Vague shadow of surmise,
Flits across her bosom young
Of a joy apart from thee,
Free be she, fancy-free,
Do not thou detain a hem,
Nor the palest rose she flung
From her summer diadem.

Though thou loved her as thyself,
As a self of purer clay,
Tho' her parting dims the day,
Stealing grace from all alive,
Heartily know,
When half-gods go,
The gods arrive.

# Lao Tse

## *from* Tao Te Ching

I have three treasures, which I hold and keep safe:
The first is called love;
The second is called moderation;
The third is called not venturing to go ahead of the world.
Being loving, one can be brave;
Being moderate, one can be ample;
Not venturing to go ahead of the world, one can be the chief of all
    officials.
Instead of love, one has only bravery;
Instead of moderation, one has only amplitude;
Instead of keeping behind, one goes ahead:
These lead to nothing but death.
For he who fights with love will win the battle;
He who defends with love will be secure.
Heaven will save him, and protect him with love.

*—from the Chinese, translated by Ch'u Ta-Kao*

# John Clare

## I Hid My Love

I hid my love when young till I
Couldn't bear the buzzing of a fly;
I hid my love to my despite
Till I could not bear to look at light:
I dare not gaze upon her face
But left her memory in each place;
Where'er I saw a wild flower lie
I kissed and bade my love good-bye.

I met her in the greenest dells,
Where dewdrops pearl the wood bluebells;
The lost breeze kissed her bright blue eye,
The bee kissed and went singing by,
A sunbeam found a passage there,
A gold chain round her neck so fair;
As secret as the wild bee's song
She lay there all the summer long.

I hid my love in field and town
Till e'en the breeze would knock me down;
The bees seemed singing ballads o'er,
The fly's bass turned to lion's roar;
And even the silence found a tongue,
To haunt me all the summer long;
The riddle nature could not prove
Was nothing else but secret love.

# Juan Ruiz

## In Praise of Love

Love to the foolish giveth wit by great and potent art,
Love to the dumb or slow of speech can eloquence impart,
Can make the craven, shrinking coward valiant and strong of
    heart,
Can by his power the sluggard spur out of his sleep to start.

Love to the young eternal youth can by his craft bestow,
The all-subduing might of eld can even overthrow;
Can make the face as swart as pitch full white and fair to
    grow,
And give to those not worth a doit full many a grace, I trow.

The dolt, the fool, the slow of wit, the poor man or the base
Unto his mistress seemeth rich in every goodly grace.
Then he that loseth lady fair should straightway set his face
Toward finding one that worthily may fill her vacant place.

*—translated from the Spanish by Ida Farnell*

# Walt Whitman

## The Last Invocation

At the last, tenderly,
From the walls of the powerful fortress'd house,
From the clasp of the knitted locks, from the keep of the
    well-closed doors,
Let me be wafted.

Let me glide noiselessly forth;
With the key of softness unlock the locks—with a whisper,
Set ope the doors, O Soul.

Tenderly—be not impatient
(Strong is your hold, O mortal flesh,
Strong is your hold, O love).


## William Shakespeare

### Sonnet CXVI


Let me not to the marriage of true minds
Admit impediments. Love is not love
Which alters when it alteration finds,
Or bends with the remover to remove:
O no! It is an ever-fixed mark,
That looks on tempests and is never shaken;
It is the star to every wand'ring bark,
Whose worth's unknown, although his height be taken.
Love's not time's fool, though rosy lips and cheeks
Within his bending sickle's compass come;
Love alters not with his brief hours and weeks,
But bears it out even to the edge of doom.
If this be error and upon me proved,
    I never writ, nor no man ever loved.

# LOVE'S DESIRES AND LONGING

## Francis Warner

### Lyric

There is no splendour in the sun
While you are absent from my arms,
And though I search till day is done
Remission in oblivion,
Watching the busy crowd go past,
Driving the brain, callousing palms,
No high philosophy rings true
Nor can contentment come, till you
Bring peace of mind, and rest at last.

## Alain Chartier

I turn you out of doors
tenant desire

you pay no rent
I turn you out of doors
all my best rooms are yours
the brain and heart

        depart
I turn you out of doors

switch off the lights
throw water on the fire
I turn you out of doors

stubborn desire

—*translated from the French by Edward Lucie-Smith*


# Christina Georgina Rossetti

## Echo


Come to me in the silence of the night;
    Come in the speaking silence of a dream;
Come with soft rounded cheeks and eyes as bright
    As sunlight on a stream;
        Come back in tears,
O memory, hope, love of finished years.

Oh dream how sweet, too sweet, too bitter sweet,
    Whose wakening should have been in Paradise,
Where souls brimfull of love abide and meet;
    Where thirsting longing eyes
        Watch the slow door
That opening, letting in, lets out no more.

Yet come to me in dreams, that I may live
    My very life again though cold in death:
Come back to me in dreams, that I may give
    Pulse for pulse, breath for breath:
        Speak low, lean low,
As long ago, my love, how long ago.

# Heinrich Heine

## Will She Come

Every morning hears me query:
    Will she come to-day?
Every evening answers, weary:
    Still she stays away.

In my nights of lonely weeping,
    Sleep I never know;
Dreaming, like a man half sleeping,
    Through the day I go.

        *—translated from the German by Ernest Beard*


# Robert Browning

## The Lost Mistress

All's over, then: does truth sound bitter
    As one at first believes?
Hark, 'tis the sparrows' good-night twitter
    About your cottage eaves!

And the leaf-buds on the vine are woolly,
    I noticed that, today;
One day more bursts them open fully
    —You know the red turns grey.

Tomorrow we meet the same then, dearest?
   May I take your hand in mine?
Mere friends are we,—well, friends the merest
   Keep much that I resign:

For each glance of the eye so bright and black.
   Though I keep with heart's endeavour,—
Your voice, when you wish the snowdrops back,
   Though it stay in my soul for ever!—

Yet I will but say what mere friends say,
   Or only a thought stronger;
I will hold your hand but as long as all may,
   Or so very little longer!

# Li Po

## A Farewell to a Friend

With a blue line of mountains north of the wall,
And east of the city a white curve of water,
Here you must leave me and drift away
Like a loosened water-plant hundreds of miles....
I shall think of you in a floating cloud;
So in the sunset think of me.
... We wave our hands to say good-bye,
And my horse is neighing again and again.

*—translated from the Chinese by Witter Bynner*

# Kālidāsa

*from* Cloud Messenger


In the twisting stream I see the play of thy eyebrows;
in the eye of the doe I see thy glance;
In the peacock's tail the luxury of thy hair.
In the moon I see the beauty of thy face,
and in the *priyāngu* I see thy slender limbs.
But ah! thy likeness united all in one place I see nowhere!
I paint thee oft as angry, red colors on smooth stones,
and would paint my own face near to thine.
But the tear rises in my eye and darkness covers my sight.
Even here [in the attempt to paint us united] our evil fate keeps us
        apart!
When the gods of the forest see me,
how I stretch out my arms to thee to draw thee to my breast,—
then, I think, from their eyes will come the tears,
which like large pearls glitter on the fresh buds.

*—translated from the Sanskrit by Max Müller*


# Lady Nakatomi


Should you refuse me
                do you think I would force you?
                no, I would remain
Confused in love as roots of rush
                and still keep longing for you

*—translated from the Japanese by Harold Wright*

# Hilary M. Freeman

*from* Days of Creation

He who drinks of Circe's wine,
Honey-ripened on the vine,
And meets the Goddess' eyes divine—
He'll never return to Ithaca.

Adrift upon the reckless sea,
Heart embracing eagerly
Its terror and its ecstasy—
He'll never return to Ithaca.

See the ivory shuttle fly,
Weaving splendour into the tapestry!
Wise Penelope will cry—
He'll never return to Ithaca.

The good ship anchored in the bay,
Tangled in her arms he lay,
Dreaming that Greece had won the day—
He'll never return to Ithaca.

For only Virtue's herb can quell,
Gift of the Gods, this binding spell ...
Unless he pass the Gates of Hell—
He'll never return to Ithaca.

# Anonymous

## Love Song

We have the utmost regard for each other at this time and place,
    but soon will be apart.
My dear whenever you gaze upon the Morning Star you will think
    of me.
When you do this it will be as if we are beholding one another.

*—translated from the Lakota (Native American)*
*by Kevin Locke*

# Suheil Bushrui

## The Wanderer

I seek a shore
as a weather-beaten sailor
lost amid the seas of the world,
searching in the folds of the wind
for a haven and a refuge
compassionate and warm
to keep the woes of life at bay.

A Sinbad am I,
the oceans are my thoughts,
the seas my feelings,
carrying me
to you
on the winds of passion
across the vast expanses of the world.

I drift on the foam,
on the crest of every wave
washed against the coastal cliffs,
the rocks of separation
on which all my ships have foundered,
their sails utterly torn
to shrouds
for lost desires.

Where are you
amid the terrible storms?
Pity me,
come forth,
make quiet approach,
carry your windblown sailor,
convey him safely ashore,
wash away his agony,
purge the wounds
of one who at your feet
bows down in meditative calm,
in sacred sanctuary.

*—translated from the Arabic by the author*

# Anonymous

*from* Karkar Island Love Song

It's been a long time since
I've seen your face sister
I have left you
For a very long time
But I still love you
And I still love you …

It is now afternoon and the place is getting dark
I sit and I think of you
Even though there is no way of me seeing you
I still love you
And I still love you

—*translated from the Takia by Alida Gubag*

# William Butler Yeats

The Lover Tells of the Rose in his Heart

All things uncomely and broken,
   all things worn out and old,
The cry of a child by the roadway,
   the creak of a lumbering cart,
The heavy steps of the ploughman,
   splashing the wintry mould,
Are wronging your image that blossoms
   a rose in the deeps of my heart.

The wrong of unshapely things
   is a wrong too great to be told;
I hunger to build them anew
   and sit on a green knoll apart,
With the earth and the sky and the water
   remade, like a casket of gold
For my dreams of your image that blossoms
   a rose in the deeps of my heart.


# Lady Kasa

Like the crane that cries
             merely to be heard afar
               in the dark of night
Must I only hear from you?
           Will we never get to meet?

          *—translated from the Japanese by Harold Wright*

37

# Torquato Tasso

## To His Mistress in Absence

Far from thy dearest self, the scope
Of all my aims,
I waste in secret flames;
And only live because I hope.

O when will Fate restore
The joys, in whose bright fire
My expectation shall expire,
That I may live because I hope no more!

*—translated from the Italian by Thomas Stanley*


# Christina Georgina Rossetti

## The First Day

I wish I could remember the first day,
First hour, first moment of your meeting me;
If bright or dim the season, it might be
Summer or winter for aught I can say.
So unrecorded did it slip away,
So blind was I to see and to foresee,
So dull to mark the budding of my tree
That would not blossom yet for many a May.

If only I could recollect it! Such
A day of days! I let it come and go
As traceless as a thaw of bygone snow.
It seemed to mean so little, meant so much!
If only now I could recall that touch,
First touch of hand in hand!—Did one but know!

# Anonymous

Through the evening mist
        there flies a flock of wild geese
           toward my loved one's home
They are calling as they fly
        and envy fills my heart

*—translated from the Japanese by Harold Wright*

# Heinrich Heine

My Heart with Hidden Tears is Swelling

My heart with hidden tears is swelling,
   I muse upon the days long gone;
The world was then a cozy dwelling,
   And people's lives flowed smoothly on.

Now all's at sixes and at sevens,
   Our life's a whirl, a strife for bread;
There is no God in all the heavens,
   And down below the Devil's dead.

And all things look so God-forsaken,
   So topsy-turvy, cold, and bare;
And if our wee bit love were taken,
   There'd be no living anywhere.

*—translated from the German by Ernest Beard*

# May Rihani

## Seven Years ... and my Love

Like mercury, like the crucified,
My love escapes compassion
And is thirsty.

Like the light at sunset,
My love carries with it the hours of the day
And hides them in the chasms of the ocean.

Like one homeless,
My love is without shelter
And the tempest buffets and assails it from all directions.

Like the Orient,
What is most beautiful about my love is the past;
And like the Orient, it knows that there will be a Resurrection.

Fresh, washed in the stream,
And carrying with it the glory of the sunrise.
What is most beautiful about my love is its promise of days to come.

*—translated from the Arabic by Suheil Bushrui*

# Hayim Nahman Bialik

### Tonight I Lurked

Tonight I lurked by your chamber
and saw you desolate and quiet;
in your eyes' searching in the window,
you sought your soul that is lost—

You looked for the reward of youth—
and didn't see, my love,
that like a frightened dove in your glass
my soul struggled and flapped.

*—translated from the Hebrew by Atar Hadari*

# Anonymous

## Love's Complaint

At wave-bright Naniwa
The sedges grow, firm-rooted—
Firm were the words you spoke,
And tender, pledging me your love,
That it would endure through all the years;
And to you I yielded my heart,
Spotless as a polished mirror.
Never, from that day, like the seaweed
That sways to and fro with the waves,
Have I faltered in my fidelity,
But have trusted in you as in a great ship.
Is it the gods who have divided us?
Is it mortal men who intervene?
You come no more, who came so often,
Nor yet arrives a messenger with your letter.
There is—alas!—nothing I can do.
Though I sorrow the black night through
And all day till the red sun sinks,
It avails me nothing. Though I pine,
I know not how to soothe my heart's pain.
Truly men call us 'weak women'.
Crying like an infant,
And lingering around, I must still wait,
Wait impatiently for a message from you!

—*translated from the Japanese by the Japanese Classics*
*Translation Committee*

# Count Aleksei Konstantinovich Tolstoy

### Believe it Not

Believe it not, when in excess of sorrow
    I murmur that my love for thee is o'er!
When ebbs the tide, think not the sea's a traitor,—
    He will return and love the land once more.

I still am pining, full of former passion:
    To thee again my freedom I'll restore,
E'en as the waves, with homeward murmur flowing,
    Roll back from far to the beloved shore!

*—translated from the Russian by John Pollen*

# Anonymous

### *from* Pleasant Songs of the Sweetheart Who Meets You in the Fields

Without your love, my heart would beat no more;
Without your love, sweet cake seems only salt;
Without your love, sweet 'shedeh' turns to bile.
O listen, darling, my heart's life needs your love;
For when you breathe, mine is the heart that beats.

*—translated from the Ancient Egyptian by Ezra Pound and Noel Stock*

# Lord Asukabe

The red leaves of oak
　　　　in the plain of Inami
　　　　　　appear in season
Yet, this longing for my love
　　　　does not have seeds in time

*—translated from the Japanese by Harold Wright*


# Francesco Petrarca

## Sonnet XIV

When welcome slumber locks my torpid frame,
I see thy spirit in the midnight dream;
Thine eyes that still in living lustre beam:
In all but frail mortality the same.
Ah! then, from earth and all its sorrows free,
Methinks I meet thee in each former scene;
Once the sweet shelter of a heart serene;
Now vocal only while I weep for thee.
For thee!—ah, no! From human ills secure.
Thy hallow'd soul exults in endless day;
'Tis I who linger on the toilsome way:
No balm relieves the anguish I endure;
Save the fond feeble hope that thou art near
To soothe my sufferings with an angel's tear.

*—translated from the Italian by Anne Bannerman*

# Anonymous

When spring arrives
                the frost on the river's moss
                        is melted away
In such a way my heart melts
                over longing for your love

—*translated from the Japanese by Harold Wright*

# LOVE'S ADORATION AND DEVOTION

## Pierre de Ronsard

### Love's Comparings

Carnations and lilies are hueless
    When set by the face of my fair,
And fine-woven gold is but worthless
    If weighted with the wealth of her hair;
      Through arches of coral passes
    Her laughter that banisheth care,
        And flowers spring fresh 'mongst the
          grasses
Wherever her feet may fare.

    *—translated from the French by Curtis Hidden Page*

# Lord Byron

## She Walks in Beauty

She walks in beauty, like the night
Of cloudless climes and starry skies;
And all that's best of dark and bright
Meet in her aspect and her eyes:
Thus mellowed to that tender light
Which heaven to gaudy day denies.

One shade the more, one ray the less,
Had half impaired the nameless grace
Which waves in every raven tress,
Or softly lightens o'er her face;
Where thoughts serenely sweet express
How pure, how dear their dwelling place.

And on that cheek, and o'er that brow,
So soft, so calm, yet eloquent,
The smiles that win, the tints that glow,
But tell of days in goodness spent,
A mind at peace with all below,
A heart whose love is innocent!

# Dante Alighieri

*from* The New Life


So gentle and so gracious doth appear
    My lady when she giveth her salute,
    That every tongue becometh, trembling, mute;
    Nor do the eyes to look upon her dare.
Although she hears her praises, she doth go
    Benignly vested with humility;
    And like a thing come down, she seems to be,
    From heaven to earth, a miracle to show.
So pleaseth she whoever cometh nigh,
    She gives the heart a sweetness through the eyes.
    Which none can understand who doth not prove.
And from her countenance there seems to move
    A spirit sweet and in Love's every guise,
    Who to the soul, in going, sayeth: Sigh!

*—translated from the Italian by Charles Eliot Norton*

# Fyodor Tyutchev

## Sunrise

The East grew white—fast flew the shallop;
   The joyous sails were full distended;
And like a heaven beneath us stretching,
   The sea with misty light was blended.

The East grew red—the maiden worshipt,
   Her veil from off her locks untying.
Heaven seemed to glow upon her features,
   As on her lips the prayer was sighing.

The East grew fire—in adoration
   She knelt, her beauteous head inclining.
And on her young cheeks, fresh and blooming,
   The tear-drops stood like jewels shining.

*—translated from the Russian by Nathan Haskell Dole*

# Háfiz

*from* The Díwán

O Beauty worshipped ever
With what sweet pain and joy,
Hid from the world's endeavour,
But seen by spirit's eye!

Alike in mosque and tavern
Thou art my only thought;
The hermit in his cavern,
He seeks what I have sought.

Belov'd, unveil the splendour
Of all the skies and spheres—
Let thy moon-face so tender
Swim through my starry tears!

—*translated from the Persian by Reynold A. Nicholson*

# Meng Jiao

Devoted Love

Chinese parasol trees become ripe and old together, side by side;
Mandarin ducks mold and die in duo, two by two;
Chaste and pure tender wife consumes and offers her life,
and gives her all to her husband, until they die;
A house and life been built and shed as such,
would not be fallen, though be hit by mighty waves;
In the heart of hers, it is a spirit, like pure water in eternal well.

*—translated from the Chinese by Ninaz Shadman*

# Kālidāsa

Lyric

Thine eyes are blue lotus flowers; thy teeth, white jasmine; thy
face is like a lotus flower. So thy body must be made of the leaves
of most delicate flowers: how comes it then that god hath given
thee a heart of stone?

My love is a hunter, who comes proudly hither. Her eyebrows
are the huntsman's bended bow; her glances are the huntsman's
piercing darts. They surely and swiftly smite my heart, which
is the wounded gazelle.

*—translated from the Sanskrit by Peter van Bohlen*

## Robert Burns

### I Love My Jean

Of a' the airts the wind can blaw,
I dearly like the west,
For there the bonnie Lassie lives,
The Lassie I lo'e best.
There wild woods grow, and rivers row,
And mony a hill's between;
But day and night my fancy's flight
Is ever wi' my Jean.

I see her in the dewy flowers,
I see her sweet and fair;
I hear her in the tunefu' birds
I hear her charm the air;
There's not a bonnie flower that springs
By fountain, shaw, or green;
There's not a bonnie bird that sings
But minds me o' my Jean.

## Anonymous

### In Praise of Love

Give me a writing board of Indian wood,
ink and a precious pen,
let me praise love for you.

It has entered my heart
forsooth, oh pupil of my eye,
you are like cool antimony.

I will care for you, come to me,
like my eldest child,
your love is not half as strong as mine.

Let me praise love for you
let me tell you what I feel,
so that you can look into my heart.

My heart is full of love,
if it had a lid,
I would open it for you.

For you I would open it,
so that you would know my love,
it is bursting my inmost being.

It is splitting my inside,
and yet I feel no pain,
so much do I love you.

Joy is the fruit of love,
when my purpose
    [to make you love me]
    is accomplished
I will give you a present for life.

I will not leave you all my life,
until death may follow,
may we live in mutual affection.

*—translated from the Swahili by Jan Knappert*

# Sir Thomas Wyatt

Alas Madam for Stealing of a Kiss

Alas! madam, for stealing of a kiss
    Have I so much your mind then offended?
Have I then done so grievously amiss,
    That by no means it may be amended?
Then revenge you, and the next way is this:
    Another kiss shall have my life ended.
For to my mouth the first my heart did suck,
The next shall clean out of my breast it pluck.


# Meleager

In the Spring a Young Man's Fancy

Now the white iris blossoms, and the rain-loving narcissus,
    And now again the lily, the mountain-roaming, blows.
Now too, the flower of lovers, the crown of all the springtime,
    Zenophila the winsome, doth blossom with the rose.
O meadows, wherefore vainly in your radiant garlands laugh ye?
    Since fairer is the maiden than any flower that grows!

*—translated from the Greek by Alma Strettell*

# Rabindranath Tagore

*from* The Gardener


Do not go, my love, without asking
my leave.
I have watched all night, and now
my eyes are heavy with sleep.
I fear lest I lose you when I'm sleeping.
Do not go, my love, without asking
my leave.
I start up and stretch my hands to
touch you. I ask myself, 'Is it a dream?'
Could I but entangle your feet with
my heart and hold them fast to my breast!
Do not go, my love, without asking
my leave.

—*translated from the Bengali by the author*

# Robert Herrick

To Anthea, who may command him Anything


Bid me to live, and I will live
    Thy Protestant to be;
Or bid me love, and I will give
    A loving heart to thee.

A heart as soft, a heart as kind,
    A heart as sound and free
As in the whole world thou canst find,
    That heart I'll give to thee.

Bid that heart stay, and it will stay
    To honour thy decree:
Or bid it languish quite away,
    And't shall do so for thee.

Bid me to weep, and I will weep
    While I have eyes to see:
And, having none, yet I will keep
    A heart to weep for thee.

Bid me despair, and I'll despair
    Under that cypress-tree:
Or bid me die, and I will dare
    E'en death to die for thee.

Thou art my life, my love, my heart,
    The very eyes of me:
And hast command of every part
    To live and die for thee.

# Anonymous

## Husband and Wife

**Wife**
While other women's husbands ride
   Along the road in proud array,
My husband up the rough hillside
   On foot must wend his weary way.

The grievous sight with bitter pain
   My bosom fills, and many a tear
Steals down my cheek, and I would fain
   Do aught to help my husband dear.

Come! take the mirror and the veil,
   My mother's parting gifts to me;
In barter they must sure avail
   To buy a horse to carry thee!

**Husband**
An I should purchase me a horse,
   Must not my wife still sadly walk?
No, no! though stony is our course,
   We'll trudge along and sweetly talk.

        *—translated from the Japanese by*
               *Basil Hall Chamberlain*

# Yehudah HaLevi

## My Sweetheart's Dainty Lips …

My sweetheart's dainty lips are red,
With ruby's crimson overspread;
Her teeth are like a string of pearls;
Down her neck her clustering curls
In ebony hue vie with the night,
And over her features dances light.

The twinkling stars enthroned above
Are sisters to my dearest love.
We men should count it joy complete
To lay our service at her feet.
But oh what rapture is her kiss!
A forecast 'tis of heavenly bliss!

*—translated from the Hebrew by Emma Lazarus*

# Francesco Petrarca

## Sonnet LXIX

Loose to the breeze her golden tresses flow'd
    Wildly in thousand mazy ringlets blown,
    And from her eyes unconquer'd glances shone,
Those glances now so sparingly bestow'd.
And true or false, meseem'd some signs she show'd
    As o'er her cheek soft pity's hue was thrown.
    I, whose whole breast with love's soft food was sown,
What wonder if at once my bosom glow'd?

Graceful she mov'd, with more than mortal mien,
In form an angel: and her accents won
Upon the ear with more than human sound.
A spirit heav'nly pure, a living sun,
Was what I saw; and if no more 'twere seen,
T' unbend the bow will never heal the wound.

*—from the Italian, translator unknown*

## Anonymous

### The Beloved

Diko,
of light skin, of smooth hair and long;
her smell is sweet and gentle
she never stinks of fish
she never breathes sweat
like gatherers of dry wood.
she has no bald patch on her head
like those who carry heavy loads.
Her teeth are white
her eyes are like
those of a new born fawn
that delights in the milk
that flows for the first time
from the antelope's udder.
Neither her heel nor her palm
are rough; but sweet to touch
like liver; or better still
the fluffy down of kapok.

*—translated from the Fulani by Ulli Beier*

# Shi Jing

## Thinking of Her

Oh, the sun of the East!
That beautiful young lady is in my chamber,
oh, she is treading the path of my footsteps,
approaching to my chamber, she is;
Oh, the moon of the East!
That pretty young lady is at the inner door of my room,
oh, she is following my footsteps,
and getting nearer, she walks away in haste.
She is the sun and the moon, rising of the East, as bright as is;
her thoughts are always, in here with me, during the day and at
     eventide.

*—translated from the Chinese by Ninaz Shadman*

# Thomas Randolph

## A Devout Lover

I have a mistress, for perfections rare
In every eye, but in my thoughts most fair.
Like tapers on the altar shine her eyes;
Her breath is the perfume of sacrifice;
And wheresoe'er my fancy would begin,
Still her perfection lets religion in.
We sit and talk, and kiss away the hours
As chastely as the morning dews kiss flowers:
I touch her, like my beads, with devout care,
And come unto my courtship as my prayer.

# Solomon

*from* The Song of Songs

Ah, you are fair, my darling,
Ah, you are fair.
Your eyes are like doves
Behind your veil.
Your hair is like a flock of goats
Streaming down Mount Gilead.
Your teeth are like a flock of ewes
Climbing up from the washing pool;
All of them bear twins,
And not one loses her young.
Your lips are like a crimson thread,
Your mouth is lovely.
Your brow behind your veil
[Gleams] like a pomegranate split open.
Your neck is like the Tower of David,
Built to hold weapons,
Hung with a thousand shields—
All the quivers of warriors.
Your breasts are like two fawns,
Twins of a gazelle,
Browsing among the lilies.
When the day blows gently
And the shadows flee,
I will betake me to the mount of myrrh,
To the hill of frankincense.
Every part of you is fair, my darling,
There is no blemish in you
From Lebanon come with me;
From Lebanon, my bride, with me!
Trip down from Amana's peak,

From the peak of Senir and Hermon,
From the dens of lions,
From the hills of leopards.

You have captured my heart,
My own, my bride,
You have captured my heart
With one [glance] of your eyes,
With one coil of your necklace.
How sweet is your love,
My own, my bride!
How much more delightful your love than wine,
Your ointments more fragrant
Than any spice!
Sweetness drops
From your lips, O bride;
Honey and milk
Are under your tongue;
And the scent of your robes
Is like the scent of Lebanon.
A garden locked
Is my own, my bride,
A fountain locked,
A sealed-up spring.
Your limbs are an orchard of pomegranates
And of all luscious fruits,
Of henna and of nard—
Nard and saffron,
Fragrant reed and cinnamon,
With all aromatic woods,
Myrrh and aloes—
All the choice perfumes.
[You are] a garden spring,

A well of fresh water,
A rill of Lebanon.

Awake, O north wind,
Come, O south wind!
Blow upon my garden,
That its perfume may spread.
Let my beloved come to his garden
And enjoy its luscious fruits!

*—translated from the Hebrew by the
Jewish Publication Society*

# Giacomo Leopardi

## To His Love

Loved beauty, who afar,
Or hiding thy sweet face,
Inspirest me with amorous delight,
Unless in slumberous night,
A sacred shade my dreamy visions trace
Or when the day doth grace
Our verdant meads and fair is Nature's smile:
The age, devoid of guile,
Perchance thou blessedst, which we golden style,
And now amid the race
Of men thou fliest, light as shadows are,
Ethereal soul? Or did beguiling Fate
Bid thee, veiled from our eyes, the future times await?

To gaze on thee alive
The hope henceforth is flown,
Unless that time when naked and alone
Upon new paths unto a dwelling strange
My spirit shall proceed. When dawn did rive
The early clouds of my tempestuous day,
Methought thou wouldst upon earth's barren soil
Be the companion of mine arduous range.
But there is nought we on our globe survey
Resembling thee; and if with careful toil
We could discover any like to thee,
She would less beauteous be,
Though much of thine in face, in limb, and voice we'd see.

Amid the floods of woe
That Fate hath given to our years below,
If son of man thy beauty did adore,
Even such as I conceive it in my mind,
He would existence, so unblessed before,
Sweet and delightful find;
And clearly doth to me my spirit tell
That I to praise and glory would aspire,
As in mine early years, for love of thee.
But Heaven hath not deemed well
To grant a solace to our misery;
And linked to thee, existence would acquire
Such beauty as on high doth bless the heavenly choir.

Amid the shady vale
Where sounds the rustic song
Of the laborious tiller of the soil,
Where seated I bewail
The youthful error that was with me long,
But now doth far recoil;
And on the hills where I, remembering, weep
The lost desires and the departed hope
Of my sad days, the thought of thee doth keep
My heart from death, and gives life further scope.
Could I in this dark age and evil air,
Preserve thine image in my soul most deep,
'Twere joy enough, for truth can never be our share.

If an eternal thought
Thou art, whom ne'er with mortal, fragile frame
Eternal Wisdom suffers to be fraught,
Or to become the prey
Of all the sorrows of death-bringing life;
Or if another globe,
Amid the innumerable worlds that flame
On high when Night displays her dusky robe,
Thy beauty doth convey;
Or star, near neighbour of the sun, doth leave
Its light on thee while gentler breezes play:
From where the days are short and dark with strife,
This hymn of an unknown adorer, oh receive!

*—translated from the Italian by Francis Henry Cliffe*

# Samuel Ibn Nagrela

## One Heart Rejoined

The flame of love is kindled
Within me—how shall I contain it?
It is destroying me
For it waits in ambush close by.
It attacks me like the Sabeans
And burns with fierce anger
As it pierces my heart.

My tears that flow by day
Reveal my inmost secrets
What will ye say to my beloved?
'Tears do not prove me right.'
How else can I be justified?

In my name speak to him
The words I have uttered:
'Do not be indifferent to me!'
Remove from my heart the injury
Made by the rupture of our love.

Comfort, comfort me,
For my insides are groaning,
Because of the pain that increases,
Even sleep is distant from me;
It eludes me and removes itself.

The hearts that were severed
Cried out to each other and embraced again.
They urged me as well
To hold him close,

To kiss and be reunited.
This poem, my love, is witness
(Like the words of a maiden singing).
Respond to its lay of friendship
That two sections of one heart rejoined shall not
    again be sundered.

*—translated from the Hebrew by Leon J. Weinberger*

# LOVE'S DELIRIUM

## William Shakespeare

*from* A Midsummer Night's Dream

More strange than true: I never may believe
These antique fables, nor these fairy toys.
Lovers and madmen have such seething brains,
Such shaping fantasies, that apprehend
More than cool reason ever comprehends.
The lunatic, the lover and the poet
Are of imagination all compact:
One sees more devils than vast hell can hold,
That is the madman: the lover, all as frantic,
Sees Helen's beauty in a brow of Egypt:
The poet's eye, in a fine frenzy rolling,
Doth glance from heaven to earth, from earth to heaven;
And as imagination bodies forth
The forms of things unknown, the poet's pen
Turns them to shapes, and gives to airy nothing
A local habitation and a name.

# Juan Ruiz

## Lament of a Despised Lover

Say, lovelorn heart, that art condemned upon despair to feed,
Why slay the form wherein thou dwellst and make it pine
    and bleed?
Why serve a lady who of love taketh but little heed?
Alas, poor heart, thy fault, I trow, thou'lt rue in very deed!

Ye weeping eyes with beauty dimmed, unhappy was the day
When first toward a lady false ye let your glances stray.
Methinketh for such grievous fault ye will full dearly pay,
And tears will rob you of your light, and take your pride
    away.

Alas, thou hapless, foolish tongue, oh say, why wast thou gain
To speak with her, that ever held thy words in proud dis-
    dain?
From one thus reckless of thy woe what thoughtest thou to
    gain?
And thou, poor tortured body, thou art wasted with thy pain.

*—translated from the Spanish by Ida Farnell*


# Anonymous

## How Well She Knows to Cast the Noose

How well she knows to cast the noose,
And yet not pay the cattle tax!
She casts the noose on me with her hair,
She captures me with her eye;
She curbs me with her necklace,
She brands me with her seal ring.

*—translated from the Ancient Egyptian by Miriam Lichtheim*

# Ernest Dowson

Nom Sum Qualis Eram Bonae Sub Regno Cynarae

Last night, ah, yesternight, betwixt her lips and mine
There fell thy shadow, Cynara! thy breath was shed
Upon my soul between the kisses and the wine;
And I was desolate and sick of an old passion,
    Yea, I was desolate and bowed my head:
I have been faithful to thee, Cynara! in my fashion.

All night upon mine heart I felt her warm heart beat,
Night-long within mine arms in love and sleep she lay;
Surely the kisses of her bought red mouth were sweet;
But I was desolate and sick of an old passion,
    When I awoke and found the dawn was gray:
I have been faithful to thee, Cynara! in my fashion.

I have forgot much, Cynara! gone with the wind,
Flung roses, roses, riotously with the throng,
Dancing, to put thy pale lost lilies out of mind;
But I was desolate and sick of an old passion,
    Yea, all the time, because the dance was long:
I have been faithful to thee, Cynara! in my fashion.

I cried for madder music and for stronger wine,
But when the feast is finished and the lamps expire,
Then falls thy shadow, Cynara! the night is thine;
And I am desolate and sick of an old passion,
    Yea, hungry for the lips of my desire:
I have been faithful to thee, Cynara! in my fashion.

# Anonymous

## Mass of Love

Dawn of a bright June morning,
    The birthday of Saint John,
When ladies and their lovers
    To hear High Mass are gone.

Yonder goes my lady,
    Among them all, the best;
In colored silk mantilla
    And many skirts she's dressed.

Embroidered is her bodice
    With gems of pearl and gold.
Her lips of beauty rare
    Beguiling sweetness hold.

Faint on the touch of rouge
    On cheeks of fairest white,
Sparkling blue her eyes
    With subtle art made bright.

Proudly church she entered
    Radiant as sun above,
Ladies died of envy
    And courtiers, of love.

A singer in the choir
    His place lost in the creed;
The priest who read the lesson
    The pages did not heed,

And acolytes beside him
   No order could restore;
Instead of Amen, Amen,
   They sang *Amor, Amor*.

      *—translated from the Spanish by Ana Pursche*


# Johann Wolfgang von Goethe

Restless Love


Through rain, through snow,
Through tempest go!
'Mongst steaming caves,
O'er misty waves,
On, on! still on!
Peace, rest have flown.

Sooner through sadness
   I'd wish to be slain,
Than all the gladness
   Of life to sustain;
All the fond yearning
   That heart feels for heart,
Only seems burning
   To make them both smart.

How shall I fly?
Forestwards hie?
Vain were all strife!
Bright crown of life,
Turbulent bliss,—
Love, thou art this!

   *—translated from the German by E.A. Bowering*

# Dante Alighieri

*from* The New Life

Within her eyes my lady beareth Love,
        So that whom she regards is gentle made;
        All toward her turn, where'er her steps are stayed,
        And whom she greets, his heart doth trembling move;
So that with face cast down, all pale to view,
        For every fault of his he then doth sigh;
        Anger and pride away before her fly:—
        Assist me, dames, to pay her honor due.
All sweetness truly, every humble thought,
        The heart of him who hears her speak doth hold;
        Whence he is blessed who hath seen her erewhile.
What seems she when a little she doth smile
        Cannot be kept in mind, cannot be told.
        Such strange and gentle miracle is wrought.

*—translated from the Italian by Charles Eliot Norton*

# Diarmad O'Curnain

Love's Despair

I know not night from day,
        Nor thrush from cuckoo gray,
Nor cloud from the sun that shines above thee—
        Nor freezing cold from heat,
        Nor friend—if friend I meet—
I but know—heart's love!—I love thee.

Love that my Life began,
Love, that will close life's span,
Love that grows ever by love-giving:
Love, from the first to last,
Love, till all life be passed,
Love that loves on after living!

*—translated from the Gaelic (Irish) by George Sigerson*

## Anacreon

### The Wounded Cupid

Cupid as he lay among
Roses, by a Bee was stung.
Whereupon in anger flying
To his Mother, said thus crying;
Help! O help! your Boy's a dying.
And why, my pretty Lad, said she?
Then blubbering, replied he,
A winged Snake has bitten me
Which Country people call a Bee.
At which she smil'd; then with her hairs
And kisses drying up his tears:
Alas! said she, my Wag! if this
Such a pernicious torment is:
Come, tell me then, how great's the smart
Of those, thou woundest with thy Dart!

*—translated from the Greek by Robert Herrick*

# Walt Whitman

## When I Heard at the Close of the Day

When I heard at the close of the day how my name had been
　　receiv'd with plaudits in the capitol, still it was not a happy
　　night for me that follow'd,
And else, when I carous'd, or when my plans were accomplish'd,
　　still I was not happy,
But the day when I rose at dawn from the bed of perfect health,
　　refresh'd, singing, inhaling the ripe breath of autumn,
When I saw the full moon in the west grow pale and disappear in
　　the morning light,
When I wander'd alone over the beach, and undressing, bathed,
　　laughing with the cool waters, and saw the sun rise,
And when I thought how my dear friend, my lover, was on his way
　　coming, O then I was happy,
O then each breath tasted sweeter, and all that day my food
　　nourish'd me more, and the beautiful day pass'd well,
And the next came with equal joy, and with the next at evening
　　came my friend,
And that night while all was still I heard the waters roll slowly
　　continually up the shores,
I heard the hissing rustle of the liquid and sands as directed to me
　　whispering to congratulate me,
For the one I love most lay sleeping by me under the same cover in
　　the cool night,
In the stillness in the autumn moonbeams his face was inclined
　　toward me,
And his arm lay lightly around my breast—and that night I was
　　happy.

# Maxamed Xaashi Dhamac 'Gaarriye'

## Passing Cloud

Setting sun
You're on the run:
Late afternoon
And gone so soon!
What are you scared of? What's the rush?
Is it the spears of light that shine
Back at you from rock and bush?
Is it the dark creeping up on you
Or bad news from the depths of night
That makes you want to hide your light?
Or is it this girl, more beautiful
Than rain the season of drought, whose grace
Is greater by far than the subtle pace
Of a passing cloud when it's nudged by the wind?
When you and she exchanged glances just now,
It was you who grew pale, it was you who shrank
From the gleam in her eye and the glow of her smile.
Setting sun
You're on the run:
Late afternoon
And gone so soon!
Have you gone
To warn the moon
That she must face
This greater grace?
The roll of the clouds, the furl of the waves—
A sea of cloud stained purple and red,
The swing of her arms, the swing and the sway
Of her hips as she walks is just like the way
You sway and dip and the end of the day.

Now the clouds turn their backs on you.
They only have eyes for the eyes of the girl:
Eyes that launch love-darts, darts that sink
Into the flanks of the clouds and draw
Droplets of blood that stain the sky.
Setting sun
You're on the run:
Late afternoon
And gone so soon...
These are the lines
That seemed to fall
To hand when first
I saw the girl.
Now this is what
I most recall:
The way she reached up to gather fruit
Believing herself to be alone
Until she saw me there, wide-eyed,
As the wind read my mind and set a gust
To part her dress and lay her breast
Bare for the space of an indrawn breath.
Ah, yes, I remember that ... and the way
She caught at the cloth and fastened it,
Turning her face from mine, her eyes
Lowered, as if to say: No man
Has seen before what you saw today.

—*translated from the Somali by David Harsent*

# Jalálu'ddín Rúmí

*from* Díwán-i Shams-i Tabríz

Happy the moment when we are seated in the palace, thou and I,
With two forms and with two figures but with one soul, thou and I.
The colours of the grove and the voice of the birds will bestow
    immortality
At the time when we come into the garden, thou and I.
The stars of heaven will come to gaze upon us:
We shall show them the moon herself, thou and I.
Thou and I, individuals no more, shall be mingled in ecstasy,
Joyful and secure from foolish babble, thou and I.
All the bright-plumed birds of heaven will devour their hearts with
    envy
In the place where we shall laugh in such a fashion, thou and I.
This is the greatest wonder, that thou and I, sitting here in the
    same nook,
Are at this moment both in 'Irák and Khurásán, thou and I.

*—translated from the Persian by Reynold A. Nicholson*

# Francesco Petrarca

## Sonnet XXVIII

Alone, and lost in thought, the desert glade
Measuring I roam with lingering steps and slow;
And still a watchful glance around me throw,
Anxious to shun the print of human tread:
No other means I find, no surer aid
From the world's prying eye to hide my woe:
So well my wild disordered gestures show,
And love-lorn looks, the fire within me bred,
That well I think each mountain, wood and plain,
And river knows, what I from man conceal,
What dreary hues my life's fool chances dim.
Yet whatever wild or savage paths I've taken,
Wherever I wander, love attends me still,
Soft whisp'ring to my soul, and I to him.

*—from the Italian, translator unknown*

# Sappho

## Love

To me he seems like a god
as he sits facing you and
hears you near as you speak
softly and laugh

in a sweet echo that jolts
the heart in my ribs. For now
as I look at you my voice
is empty and

can say nothing as my tongue
cracks and slender fire is quick
under my skin. My eyes are dead
to light, my ears

pound, and sweat pours over me.
I convulse, paler than grass,
and feel my mind slip as I
go close to death.

—*translated from the Greek by Willis Barnstone*

# Imra'u'l-Kais

*from* The Mu'allakát

Fair white arms shall she show, as a white she-camel's
Pure as her's the long-necked one, yet unmounted.
Twin breasts smooth, shalt thou see, as of ivory polished,
Guarded close from the eyes, the hands of lovers.
Waist how supple, how slim! Thou shalt span it sweetly;
Fair flanks sloped to thine eyes and downward bending.
Broad her hips for desire, than thy tent door wider;
Nay, but thine is her waist, thine own for madness.

*—translated from the Arabic by Lady Anne Blunt*
*and Wilfrid Scawen Blunt*


# Ibycus

Love Knows No Winter Sleep

In spring the quince trees
ripen in the girls' holy orchard
with river waters;
and grapes turn violet
under the shade of luxuriant leafage
and newborn shoots.

But for me, Eros
knows no winter sleep, and as north winds
burn down from Thrace
with searing lightning,
Kypris mutilates my heart with black
and baleful love.

*—translated from the Greek by Willis Barnstone*

# Firdausí

*from* The Sháhnáma


Manízha, when the time drew nigh
For parting, fain would rest her eye
On Bízhan. When she saw him sad,
She called her handmaidens and bade
Them mingle in the wine's sweet draught
A drug that steals the sense. By craft
They gave it him, and as he drank,
His head inebriated sank.
Straight she prepared a palanquin,
The sleeping youth was laid within.
On one side was a pleasure-seat,
A couch on the other, all complete
Of sandal-wood. She sprinkled there
Camphor and shed the rose-water.
Soon as they neared Turania's town
She wrapped him in a hooded gown,
And entered secretly at night
The palace—none but friends knew how—
Made ready a chamber of delight,
And eager for his waking now,
Poured in his ear a medicine
That quickly the dulled sense uncharms:
He woke and found the jessamine
Sweet-bosomed lady in his arms.
Afrásiyáb's palace! In duress,
And bowered with the fair princess.

—*translated from the Persian by Reynold A. Nicholson*

# Anonymous

## My Heart Flutters Hastily

My heart flutters hastily,
When I think of my love of you;
It lets me not act sensibly,
It leaps from its place.
It lets me not put on a dress,
Nor wrap my scarf around me;
I put no paint upon my eyes,
I'm even not anointed.
'Don't wait, go there,' says it to me,
As often as I think of him;
My heart, don't act so stupidly,
Why do you play the fool?
Sit still, the brother comes to you,
And many eyes as well.
Let not the people say of me:
'A woman fallen through love!'
Be steady when you think of him,
My heart, do not flutter!

*—translated from the Ancient Egyptian by*
*Miriam Lichtheim*

# THE JOYS AND PLEASURES OF LOVE

## William Morris

Love is Enough

Love is enough: though the World be a-waning,
And the woods have no voice but the voice of complaining,
    Though the sky be too dark for dim eyes to discover
The gold-cups and daisies fair blooming thereunder,
Though the hills be held shadows, and the sea a dark wonder,
    And this day draw a veil over all deeds pass'd over,
Yet their hands shall not tremble, their feet shall not falter;
The void shall not weary, the fear shall not alter
    These lips and these eyes of the loved and the lover.

# Charles Baudelaire

Invitation to the Voyage

My child, my sister,
Think of the rapture
Of living together there!
Of loving at will,
Of loving till death,
In the land that is like you!
The misty sunlight
Of those cloudy skies
Has for my spirit the charms,
So mysterious,
Of your treacherous eyes,
Shining brightly through their tears.

There all is order and beauty,
Luxury, peace, and pleasure.

Gleaming furniture,
Polished by the years,
Will ornament our bedroom;
The rarest flowers
Mingling their fragrance
With the faint scent of amber,
The ornate ceilings,
The limpid mirrors,
The oriental splendor,
All would whisper there
Secretly to the soul
In its soft, native language.

There all is order and beauty,
Luxury, peace, and pleasure.

See on the canals
Those vessels sleeping.
Their mood is adventurous;
It's to satisfy
Your slightest desire
That they come from the ends of the earth.
—The setting suns
Adorn the fields,
The canals, the whole city,
With hyacinth and gold;
The world falls asleep
In a warm glow of light.

There all is order and beauty,
Luxury, peace, and pleasure.

*—translated from the French by William Aggeler*

# Ahli of Shíráz

*from* Sham' u Parwana


Happy the lover in whose generous fancy
His heart is the moth of the candle of beauty.
There flutters a moth in his bosom each evening:
Night finds him candle-like with burning heart waking.
Through his grief his heart like a burnt moth is tattered,
Like a candle his skirt with his tears is watered.
One may set to his heart, like a lantern, a brand,
That enflames his whole bosom at touch of the hand.
Of a kindling let no living heart be bereft,
Of what use is a candle that unlit is left?

*—translated from the Persian by Reuben Levy*

# Christopher Marlowe

## The Passionate Shepherd to His Love

Come live with me and be my love,
And we will all the pleasures prove
That valleys, groves, hills, and fields,
Woods, or steepy mountain yields.

And we will sit upon the rocks,
Seeing the shepherds feed their flocks,
By shallow rivers to whose falls
Melodious birds sing madrigals.

And I will make thee beds of roses
And a thousand fragrant posies,
A cap of flowers, and a kirtle
Embroidered all with leaves of myrtle;

A gown made of the finest wool
Which from our pretty lambs we pull;
Fair lined slippers for the cold,
With buckles of the purest gold;

A belt of straw and ivy buds,
With coral clasps and amber studs:
And if these pleasures may thee move,
Come live with me and be my love.

The shepherds' swains shall dance and sing
For thy delight each May morning:
If these delights thy mind may move,
Then live with me and be my love.

# Juan Melendez Valdes

Of Love's Awakening


When I was yet a child,
  A child Dorila too,
To gather there the flowerets wild,
  We roved the forest through.

And gaily garlands then,
  With passing skill displayed,
To crown us both, in childish vein,
  Her little fingers made.

And thus our joys to share,
  In such our thoughts and play,
We passed along, a happy pair,
  The hours and days away.

But e'en in sports like these,
  Soon age came hurrying by!
And of our innocence the ease
  Malicious seemed to fly.

I knew not how it was,
  To see me she would smile;
And but to speak to her would cause
  Me pleasure strange the while.

Then beat my heart the more,
  When flowers to her I brought;
And she, to wreathe them as before,
  Seemed silent, lost in thought.

One evening after this
    We saw two turtle-doves,
With trembling throat, who, wrapt in bliss,
    Were wooing in their loves.

In manifest delight,
    With wings and feathers bowed,
Their eyes fixed on each other bright,
    They languished, moaning loud.

The example made us bold,
    And with a pure caress,
The troubles we had felt we told,
    Our pains and happiness.

And at once from our view
    Then, like a shadow, fled
Our childhood and its joys, but new,
    Love gave us his instead.

*—translated from the Spanish by James Kennedy*

# Dante Gabriel Rossetti

## Sudden Light

I have been here before,
   But when or how I cannot tell:
I know the grass beyond the door,
   The sweet keen smell,
The sighing sound, the lights around the shore.

You have been mine before,—
   How long ago I may not know:
But just when at that swallow's soar
   Your neck turned so,
Some veil did fall,—I knew it all of yore.

Has this been thus before?
   And shall not thus time's eddying flight
Still with our lives our love restore
   In death's despite,
And day and night yield one delight once more?

# Zheng Jiuling

## Dark Night's Moon

Bright moon rises over the ocean,
when joining with heaven in light, within the horizon;
When the hearts of lovers are fallen apart,
and long night's darkness causes tender thoughts;
Though the candle light is blown and withered,
it is not darker, the grave of the night;

Though I wear a mantle over my heavy robe,
yet, the chilling dews make it no warmer;
Restlessly favoring a present, a trust, to the moon,
I return to sleep, yearning for dreams, excellent and sweet!

*—translated from the Chinese by Ninaz Shadman*

## Solomon Ibn Gabirol

### For a Marriage

Send to the prince's daughter
    Her ruddy, fair-eyed king,
Like a fruitful branch he blossoms,
    Transplanted to a spring.

Thy Torah has his worship,
    He runs, to taste its charms,
Before Thee like a warrior,
    Accoutred in his arms.

I day by day am waiting
    Salvation's promised day,
Enquiring how and whence it
    Will come to be my stay.

Restore the tortured People
    To the friend of her youth divine,
And bring the two together
    To the house of joy and wine.

*—translated from the Hebrew by Israel Zangwill
    for the Jewish Publication Society of America*

# Edmund Spenser

*from* The Fairy Queen

Great Venus! Queen of Beauty and of Grace!
   The Joy of Gods and men! that under sky
Dost fairest shine, and most adorn thy place:
   That, with thy smiling look, dost pacify
   The raging seas, and mak'st the storms to fly;
Thee, Goddess! thee, the winds, the clouds, do fear:
   And when thou spread'st thy mantle forth on high,
The waters play, and pleasant lands appear,
And heavens laugh, and all the world shows joyous cheer.

Then doth the dædale earth throw forth to thee
   Out of her fruitful lap abundant flowers:
And then all living wights, soon as they see
   The spring break forth out of his lusty bowers,
   They all do learn to play the paramours;
First do the merry birds, thy pretty pages,
   Privily picked with thy lustful powers,
Chirp loud to thee out of their leafy cages,
And thee their mother call to cool their kindly rages.

Then do the savage beasts begin to play
   Their pleasant frisks, and loathe their wonted food;
The lions roar; the tigers loudly bray;
   The raging bulls re-bellow through the wood,
   And breaking forth, dare tempt the deepest flood
To come where thou dost draw them with desire.
   So all things else, that nourish vital blood,
Soon as with fury thou dost them inspire,
In generation seek to quench their inward fire.

So all the world by thee at first was made,
    And daily yet thou dost the same repair:
Ne ought on earth that merry is and glad,
    Ne ought on earth that merry is and glad,
    But thou the same for pleasure didst prepare.
Thou art the root of all that joyous is:
    Great god of men and women, queen of the air,
Mother of laughter, and well-spring of bliss,
O grant that of my love at last I may not miss!

# Kahlil Gibran

*from* The Prophet

All these things shall love do unto you that you may know the secrets
of your heart, and in that knowledge become a fragment of Life's
heart.

But if in your fear you would seek only love's peace and love's pleasure,
Then it is better for you that you cover your nakedness and pass out of
      love's threshing-floor,
Into the seasonless world where you shall laugh, but not all of your
      laughter, and weep, but not all of your tears.

Love gives naught but itself and takes naught but from itself.
Love possesses not nor would it be possessed;
For love is sufficient unto love.

When you love you should not say, 'God is in my heart,' but rather, 'I
      am in the heart of God.'
And think not you can direct the course of love, for love, if it finds you
      worthy, directs your course.

Love has no other desire but to fulfill itself.
But if you love and must needs have desires, let these be your desires:
To melt and be like a running brook that sings its melody to the night.
To know the pain of too much tenderness.
To be wounded by your own understanding of love;
And to bleed willingly and joyfully.
To wake at dawn with a winged heart and give thanks for another day of
      loving;
To rest at the noon hour and meditate love's ecstasy;
To return home at eventide with gratitude;
And then to sleep with a prayer for the beloved in your heart and a song
      of praise upon your lips.

# San Juan de la Cruz

## Living Flame of Love

O living flame of love
That, burning, dost assail
My inmost soul with tenderness untold,
Since thou dost freely move,
Deign to consume the veil
Which sunders this sweet converse that we hold.

O burn that searest never!
O wound of deep delight!
O gentle hand! O touch of love supernal
That quick'nest life for ever,
Putt'st all my woes to flight,
And, slaying, changest death to life eternal!

And O, ye lamps of fire,
In whose resplendent light
The deepest caverns where the senses meet,
Erst steep'd in darkness dire,
Blaze with new glories bright
And to the lov'd one give both light and heat!

How tender is the love
Thou wak'nest in my breast
When thou, alone and secretly, art there!
Whispering of things above,
Most glorious and most blest,
How delicate the love thou mak'st me bear!

*—translated from the Spanish by E. Allison Peers*

# George Meredith

*from* Love in the Valley

Under yonder beech-tree single on the green-sward,
Couched with her arms behind her golden head,
Knees and tresses folded to slip and ripple idly,
Lies my young love sleeping in the shade.
Had I the heart to slide an arm beneath her,
Press her parting lips as her waist I gather slow,
Waking in amazement she could not but embrace me:
Then would she hold me and never let me go?

Shy as the squirrel and wayward as the swallow,
Swift as the swallow along the river's light
Circleting the surface to meet his mirrored winglets,
Fleeter she seems in her stay than in her flight.
Shy as the squirrel that leaps among the pine-tops,
Wayward as the swallow overhead at set of sun,
She whom I love is hard to catch and conquer,
Hard, but O the glory of the winning were she won!

\* \* \*

Hither she comes; she comes to me; she lingers,
Deepens her brown eyebrows, while in new surprise
High rise the lashes in wonder of a stranger;
Yet am I the light and living of her eyes.
Something friends have told her fills her heart to brimming,
Nets her in her blushes, and wounds her, and tames.—
Sure of her haven, O like a dove alighting,
Arms up, she dropped: our souls were in our names.

# Heinrich Heine

*from* Homeward Bound

Thou fairest fisher maiden,
    Row thy boat to the land.
Come here and sit beside me,
    Whispering, hand in hand.

Lay thy head on my bosom,
    And have no fear of me;
For carelessly thou trustest
    Daily the savage sea.

My heart is like the ocean,
    With storm and ebb and flow,
And many a pearl lies hidden,
    Within its depths below.

*—translated from the German by Emma Lazarus*

# Ben Jonson

## Song: To Celia

Drink to me only with thine eyes,
And I will pledge with mine;
Or leave a kiss but in the cup,
And I'll not look for wine.
The thirst that from the soul doth rise,
Doth ask a drink divine:
But might I of Jove's nectar sup,
I would not change for thine.
I sent thee late a rosy wreath,
Not so much honoring thee,
As giving it a hope, that there
It could not withered be.
But thou thereon did'st only breathe,
And sent'st it back to me;
Since when it grows and smells, I swear,
Not of itself, but thee!


# Anonymous

## *from* Love Lyrics

To have seen her
To have seen her approaching
Such beauty is
Joy in my heart forever.
Nor time eternal take back
What she has brought to me.

—*translated from the Ancient Egyptian by Ezra Pound and Noel Stock*

# Paul Laurence Dunbar

## Love's Draft

The draft of love was cool and sweet
You gave me in the cup,
But, ah, love's fire is keen and fleet,
And I am burning up.
Unless the tears I shed for you
Shall quench this burning flame,
It will consume me through and through,
And leave but ash—a name.

# Apollon Nikolayvich Maykov

## The Kiss Refused

I would kiss you, lover true!
    But I fear the moon would spy;
Little bright stars watch us too.
    Little stars might fall from sky
To the blue sea, telling all!
To the oars the sea will tell,
    Oars, in turn, tell Fisher Eno—
Him whom Mary loveth well:
And when Mary knows a thing,
    All the neighborhood will know;—
How by moonlight in the garden
    Where the fragrant flowers grow,
I caressed and fondly kissed thee,
    While the silver apple-tree
    Shed its bloom on you and me!

                    —*translated from the Russian by John Pollen*

# Anonymous

*from* The Crossing


I dwell upon your love
   through the night and all
the day, through the hours
   I lie asleep and when
I wake again at dawn.

Your beauty nourishes hearts.
   Your voice creates desire.
It makes my body strong.
   '…he is weary …'
So may I say whenever …
   There is no other girl
in harmony with his heart.
   I am the only one.

      *—translated from the Ancient Egyptian by*
             *Barbara Hughes Fowler*

# John Millington Synge

## The Meeting

We met among the furze in golden mist,
Watching a golden moon that filled the sky,
And there my lips your lips' young glory kissed
Till old high loves, in our high love went by.

Then in the hush of plots with shining trees
We lay like gods disguised in shabby dress,
Making with birches, bracken, stars and seas,
Green courts of pleasure for each long caress;
Till there I found in you and you in me
The crowns of Christ and Eros—all divinity.

# THE SORROWS AND PAIN OF LOVE

## Percy Bysshe Shelley

*from* Epipsychidion

… Love's very pain is sweet,
But its reward is in the world divine,
Which, if not here, it builds beyond the grave …

## Johann Wolfgang von Goethe

*from* The West-Eastern Divan

Love wrought on me with evil mind!
That in good truth I well may say;
I sing indeed with heavy heart.
But see these tapers—'tis their part
To shine even while they waste away.

Love's anguish sought a place apart,
    Where all was desolate, wild and rude;
He found betimes my empty heart,
    And nested in the solitude.

—*translated from the German by Edward Dowden*

# Dame Edith Sitwell

*from* Heart and Mind

Said the Sun to the Moon—'When you are but a lonely white crone,
And I, a dead King in my golden armour somewhere in a dark wood,
Remember only this of our hopeless love:
That never till Time is done
Will the fire of the heart and the fire of the mind be one.'

# Francesco Petrarca

Sonnet XIII

If the lorn bird complain, or rustling sweep
  Soft summer airs o'er foliage waving slow,
  Or the hoarse brook come murmuring down the steep,
  Where on the enamel'd bank I sit below
With thoughts of love that bid my numbers flow;
  'Tis then I see her, though in earth she sleep!
  *Her*, form'd in Heaven! I see, and hear, and know!
  Responsive sighing, weeping as I weep:
  'Alas!' she pitying says, 'ere yet the hour,
  Why hurry life away with swifter flight?
  Why from thy eyes this flood of sorrow pour?
No longer mourn my fate! through death my days
  Become eternal! to eternal light
  These eyes which seem'd in darkness closed, I raise!'

*—translated from the Italian by Barbarina Dacre*

# Hartley Coleridge

Early Death

She pass'd away like morning dew
    Before the sun was high;
So brief her time, she scarcely knew
    The meaning of a sigh.

As round the rose its soft perfume,
    Sweet love around her floated;
Admired she grew—while mortal doom
    Crept on, unfear'd, unnoted.

Love was her guardian Angel here,
    But Love to Death resign'd her;
Tho' love was kind, why should we fear
    But holy Death is kinder.


# Sa'dí of Shíráz

*from* The Preface to the Rose-Garden

Ask me not His description! Nay, for how,
How might I senseless of the Signless speak?
We lovers are the slain of the Beloved,
'Tis idle of the slain a voice to seek.

—*translated from the Persian by Reynold A. Nicholson*

# Charles Baudelaire

## The Death of Lovers

We shall have beds full of subtle perfumes,
Divans as deep as graves, and on the shelves
Will be strange flowers that blossomed for us
Under more beautiful heavens.

Using their dying flames emulously,
Our two hearts will be two immense torches
Which will reflect their double light
In our two souls, those twin mirrors.

Some evening made of rose and of mystical blue
A single flash will pass between us
Like a long sob, charged with farewells;

And later an Angel, setting the doors ajar,
Faithful and joyous, will come to revive
The tarnished mirrors, the extinguished flames.

*—translated from the French by William Aggeler*

# Alexander Pushkin

## The Rose

Where is our rose, friends?
    Tell if ye may!
Faded the rose, friends,
    The Dawn-child of Day.
    Ah, do not say,
Such is life's fleetness!
    No, rather say,
I mourn thee, rose, —farewell!
Now to the lily-bell
    Flit we away.

—*translated from the Russian by Thomas B. Shaw*

# Anonymous

## Love Song

The body perishes, the heart stays young.
The platter wears away with serving food.
No log retains its bark when old,
No lover peaceful while the rival weeps.

—*translated from the Zulu by Ulli Beier*

# Jalálu'ddín Rúmí

Love, the Hierophant

'Tis heart-ache lays the lover's passion bare:
No sickness with heart-sickness may compare.
Love is a malady apart, the sign
And astrolabe of mysteries Divine.
Whether of heavenly mould or earthly cast,
Love still doth lead us Yonder at the last.
Reason, explaining Love, can naught but flounder
Like ass in mire: Love is Love's own expounder.
Does not the sun himself the sun declare?
Behold him! All the proof thou seek'st is there.

—*translated from the Persian by Reynold A. Nicholson*

# Homer

*from* The Odyssey

'O (she cries)
Let not against thy spouse thine anger rise!
O versed in every turn of human art,
Forgive the weakness of a woman's heart!
The righteous powers, that mortal lots dispose,
Decree us to sustain a length of woes,
And from the flower of life the bliss deny
To bloom together, fade away, and die.
O let me, let me not thine anger move,
That I forbore, thus, thus to speak my love;
Thus in fond kisses, while the transport warms,
Pour out my soul, and die within thine arms!
I dreaded fraud! Men, faithless men, betray
Our easy faith, and make the sex their prey:
Against the fondness of my heart is strove:
'Twas caution, O my lord! not want of love.
Like me had Helen fear'd, with wanton charms,
Ere the fair mischief set two worlds in arms;
Ere Greece rose dreadful in the avenging day;
Thus had she fear'd, she had not gone astray.
But Heaven, averse to Greece, in wrath decreed
That she should wander, and that Greece should bleed:
Blind to the ills that from injustice flow,
She colour'd all our wretched lives with woe.
But why these sorrows when my lord arrives?
I yield, I yield! my own Ulysses lives!
The secrets of the bridal bed are known
To thee, to me, to Actoris alone
(My father's present in the spousal hour,
The sole attendant on our genial bower).

Since what no eye hath seen thy tongue reveal'd,
Hard and distrustful as I am, I yield.'

                    —*translated from the Greek by Alexander Pope*

# Mutanabbí

*from* Díwán al-Mutanabbí

How glows mine heart for him whose heart to me is cold,
Who liketh ill my case and me in fault doth hold!
Why should I hide a love that hath worn thin my frame?
To Saifu'ddaula all the world avows the same.
Though love of his high star unites us, would that we
According to our love might so divide the fee!
Him have I visited when sword in sheath was laid,
And I have seen him when in blood swam every blade:
Him, both in peace and war the best of all mankind,
Whose crown of excellence was still his noble mind.

Do foes by flight escape thine onset, thou dost gain
A chequered victory, half of pleasure, half of pain.
So puissant is the fear thou strik'st them with, it stands
Instead of thee and works more than thy warriors' hands.
Unfought the field is thine: thou need'st not further strain
To chase them from their holes in mountain or in plain.
What! 'fore thy fierce attack whene'er an army reels,
Must thy ambitious soul press hot upon their heels?
Thy task it is to rout them on the battle-ground:
No shame to thee if they in flight have safety found.
Or thinkest thou, perchance, that victory is sweet
Only when scimitars and necks each other greet?

O justest of the just save in thy deeds to me!
*Thou* art accused and thou, O Sire, must judge the plea.
Look, I implore thee, well! Let not thine eye cajoled
See fat in empty froth, in all that glisters gold!
What use and profit reaps a mortal of his sight,
If darkness unto him be indistinct from light?

My deep poetic art the blind have eyes to see,
My verses ring in ears as deaf as deaf can be.
They wander far abroad whilst I am unaware,
But men collect them watchfully with toil and care.
Oft hath my laughing mien prolonged the insulter's sport
Until with claw and mouth I cut his rudeness short.
Ah, when the lion bares his teeth, suspect his guile,
Nor fancy that the lion shows to thee a smile!
I have slain the foe that sought my heart's blood, many a time,
Riding a noble mare whose back none else may climb,
Whose hind and fore-legs seem in galloping as one;
Nor hand nor foot requireth she to urge her on.
And oh, the days when I have swung my fine-edged glaive
Amidst a sea of death where wave was dashed on wave!
The desert knows me well, the night, the mounted men,
The battle and the sword, the paper and the pen!

*—translated from the Arabic by Reynold A. Nicholson*

# Fyodor Tyutchev

## Last Love

Love at the closing of our days
is apprehensive and very tender.
Glow brighter, brighter, farewell rays
of one last love in its evening splendor.

Blue shade takes half the world away:
through western clouds alone some light is slanted.
O tarry, O tarry, declining day,
enchantment, let me stay enchanted.

The blood runs thinner, yet the heart
remains as ever deep and tender.
O last belated love, thou art
a blend of joy and of hopeless surrender.

*—translated from the Russian by Vladimir Nabokov*


# Kahlil Gibran

*from* The Prophet

When love beckons to you, follow him,
Though his ways are hard and steep.
And when his wings enfold you yield to him,
Though the sword hidden among his pinions may wound you.
And when he speaks to you believe in him,
Though his voice may shatter your dreams as the north wind lays
    waste the garden.

For even as love crowns you so shall he crucify you. Even as he is for
  your growth so is he for your pruning.
Even as he ascends to your height and caresses your tenderest
  branches that quiver in the sun,
So shall he descend to your roots and shake them in their clinging
  to the earth.

Like sheaves of corn he gathers you unto himself.
He threshes you to make you naked.
He sifts you to free you from your husks.
He grinds you to whiteness.
He kneads you until you are pliant;
And then he assigns you to his sacred fire, that you may become
  sacred bread for God's sacred feast.

## Bhartrihari

*from* Lyric

She whom I love loves another, and the other again loves another,
  while another is pleased with me. Ah! the tricks of the god of
  love!

       *—translated from the Sanskrit by Peter van Bohlen*

# Samuel Ibn Nagrela

## One Chain of Your Neck

Beloved, will you rescue your lover captive in the pit?
Dispatch the fragrance of your garments to inform him thus!
Will you draw out your lips with waters of red tint
Or with the blood of fawns give scent to your cheeks?
Provide pleasure to your lover as reward for his ardor
And take my life and my soul as the price of your dowry!
If with your two eyes you break my heart,
But one chain of your neck will make it live again!

*—translated from the Hebrew by Leon J. Weinberger*


# Lord Byron

## When We Two Parted

When we two parted
    In silence and tears,
Half broken-hearted
    To sever for years,
Pale grew thy cheek and cold,
    Colder thy kiss;
Truly that hour foretold
    Sorrow to this.

The dew of the morning
    Sunk chill on my brow—
It felt like the warning
    Of what I feel now.
Thy vows are all broken,
    And light is thy fame;
I hear thy name spoken,
    And share in its shame.

They name thee before me,
    A knell to mine ear;
A shudder comes o'er me—
    Why wert thou so dear?
They know not I knew thee,
    Who knew thee too well—
Long, long shall I rue thee,
    Too deeply to tell.

In secret we met—
    In silence I grieve,
That thy heart could forget,
    Thy spirit deceive.
If I should meet thee
    After long years,
How should I greet thee?—
    With silence and tears.

# Pierre de Ronsard

His Lady's Tomb


As in the gardens, all through May, the rose,
Lovely and young and rich apparelled,
Makes sunrise jealous of her rosy red,
When dawn upon the dew of dawning glows;
Graces and Loves within her breast repose,
    The woods are faint with the sweet odour shed,
    Till rains and heavy suns have smitten dead
The languid flower and the loose leaves unclose:

So this, the perfect beauty of our days,
When heaven and earth were vocal of her praise,
    The fates have slain, and her sweet soul reposes:
And tears I bring, and sighs, and on her tomb
Pour milk, and scatter buds of many a bloom,
    That, dead as living, Rose may be with roses.

*—translated from the French by Andrew Lang*

# William Blake

Love's Secret

Never seek to tell thy love,
Love that never told can be;
For the gentle wind doth move
Silently, invisibly.

I told my love, I told my love,
I told her all my heart,
Trembling, cold, in ghastly fears.
Ah! She did depart!

Soon after she was gone from me,
A traveler came by,
Silently, invisibly:
He took her with a sigh.

# Alexander Pushkin

I Loved You

I loved you; even now I may confess,
    Some embers of my love their fire retain;
But do not let it cause you more distress,
    I do not want to sadden you again.
Hopeless and tonguetied, yet I loved you dearly
    With pangs the jealous and the timid know;
So tenderly I loved you, so sincerely,
    I pray God grant another love you so.

*—translated from the Russian by Reginald Mainwaring Hewitt*

# Lady Sakanoe

## A Maiden's Lament

Full oft he sware with accents true and tender,
   'Though years roll by, my love shall ne'er wax old!'
And so to him my heart I did surrender,
   Clear as a mirror of pure burnished gold;

And from that day, unlike the seaweed bending
   To every wave raised by the autumn gust,
Firm stood my heart, on him alone depending,
   As the bold seaman in his ship doth trust.

Is it some cruel god that hath bereft me?
   Or hath some mortal stolen away his heart?
No word, no letter since the day he left me;
   Nor more he cometh, ne'er again to part!

In vain I weep, in helpless, hopeless sorrow,
   From earliest morn until the close of day;
In vain, till radiant dawn brings back the morrow,
   I sigh the weary, weary nights away.

No need to tell how young I am, and slender—
   A little maid that in thy palm could lie:
Still for some message comforting and tender
   I pace the room in sad expectancy.

    —*translated from the Japanese by Basil Hall Chamberlain*

# Thomas Hardy

A Broken Appointment

You did not come,
And marching Time drew on, and wore me numb.—
Yet less for loss of your dear presence there
Than that I thus found lacking in your make
That high compassion which can overbear
Reluctance for pure loving-kindness' sake
Grieved I, when, as the hope-hour stroked its sum,
You did not come.

You love not me,
And love alone can lend you loyalty;
—I know and knew it. But, unto the store
Of human deeds divine in all but name,
Was it not worth a little hour or more
To add yet this: Once you, a woman, came
To soothe a time-torn man; even though it be
You love not me?

# Luís Vaz De Camões

*from* Rimas

Love is a fire that burns unseen,
a wound that aches yet isn't felt,
an always discontent contentment,
a pain that rages without hurting,

a longing for nothing but to long,
a loneliness in the midst of people,
a never feeling pleased when pleased,
a passion that gains when lost in thought.

It's being enslaved of your own free will;
it's counting your defeat a victory;
it's staying loyal to your killer.

But if it's so self-contradictory,
how can Love, when Love chooses,
bring human hearts into sympathy?

—*translated from the Portuguese by Richard Zenith*

# Alexander Pushkin

## To —


Yes! I remember well our meeting
    When first thou dawnèdst on my sight,
  Like some fair phantom past me fleeting,
    Some nymph of purity and light.

By weary agonies surrounded
    'Mid toil, 'mid mean and noisy care,
Long in mine ear thy soft voice sounded,
    Long dreamed I of thy features fair.

Years flew; Fate's blast grew ever stronger,
    Scattering mine early dreams to air,
And thy soft voice I heard no longer—
    No longer saw thy features fair.

In exile's silent desolation
    Slowly dragged on the days for me,—
Orphaned of life, of inspiration,
    Of tears, of love, of deity.

I woke: once more my heart was beating—
    Once more thou dawnèdst on my sight,
Like some fair phantom past me fleeting,
    Some nymph of purity and light.

My heart has found its consolation;
    All has revived once more for me,
And vanished life, and inspiration,
    And tears, and love, and deity.

*—translated from the Russian by Thomas B. Shaw*

# Edmund Waller

Song

Go, lovely Rose!
Tell her that wastes her time and me
    That now she knows,
When I resemble her to thee,
How sweet and fair she seems to be.

Tell her that's young,
And shuns to have her graces spied,
    That hadst thou sprung
In deserts, where no men abide,
Thou must have uncommended died.

Small is the worth
Of beauty from the light retired;
    Bid her come forth,
Suffer herself to be desired,
And not blush so to be admired.

Then die! that she
The common fate of all things rare
    May read in thee;
How small a part of time they share
That are so wondrous sweet and fair!

# Bhartrihari

*from* Lyric

Where thou art not and the light of thine eyes, there to me is darkness; even by the brightness of the taper's light, all to me is dark. Even by the quiet glow of the hearth-fire, all to me is dark. Though the moon and the stars shine together, yet all is dark to me. The light of the sun is able only to distress me. Where thou, my doe, and thine eyes are not, there all is dark to me.

*—translated from the Sanskrit by Von Schroeder*

# D.H. Lawrence

Intimates

Don't you care for my love? she said bitterly.

I handed her the mirror, and said:
Please address these questions to the proper person!
Please make all requests to head-quarters!
In all matters of emotional importance
please approach the supreme authority direct!—
So I handed her the mirror.

And she would have broken it over my head,
but she caught sight of her own reflection
and that held her spellbound for two seconds
while I fled.

# Paul Verlaine

You would have understood me, had you waited;
  I could have loved you, dear! as well as he:
Had we not been impatient, dear! and fated
  Always to disagree.

What is the use of speech? Silence were fitter:
  Lest we should still be wishing things unsaid.
Though all the words we ever spake were bitter,
  Shall I reproach you dead?

Nay, let this earth, your portion, likewise cover
  All the old anger, setting us apart:
Always, in all, in truth was I your lover;
  Always, I held your heart.

I have met other women who were tender,
  As you were cold, dear! with a grace as rare.
Think you, I turned to them, or made surrender,
  I who had found you fair?

Had we been patient, dear! ah, had you waited,
  I had fought death for you, better than he:
But from the very first, dear! we were fated
  Always to disagree.

Late, late, I come to you, now death discloses
  Love that in life was not to be our part:
On your low lying mound between the roses,
  Sadly I cast my heart.

I would not waken you: nay! this is fitter;
    Death and the darkness give you unto me;
Here we who loved so, were so cold and bitter,
    Hardly can disagree.

*—translated from the French by Ernest Dowson*


# Po Chu-yi

*from* The Song of Lasting Regret


'Turning my head and looking down to the sites of the mortal sphere,
I can no longer see Ch'ang-an, what I see is dust and fog.
Let me take up these familiar old objects to attest to my deep love:
The filigree case, the two-pronged hairpin of gold, I entrust to you to
    take back.

'Of the hairpin but one leg remains, and one leaf-fold of the case;
The hairpin is broken in its yellow gold, and the case's filigree halved.
But if only his heart is as enduring as the filigree and the gold,
Above in heaven, or amidst men, we shall surely see each other.'

As the envoy was to depart, she entrusted poignantly to him words as well,
Words in which there was a vow that only two hearts would know:
'On the seventh day of the seventh month, in the Hall of Protracted Life,
At the night's mid-point, when we spoke alone, with no one else around—
"In heaven, would that we might become birds of coupled wings!
On earth, would that we might be trees of intertwining limbs! …"'
Heaven is lasting, earth long-standing, but there is a season for their end;
*This* regret stretches on and farther, with no ending time.

*—translated from the Chinese by Paul W. Kroll*

# Giacomo Leopardi

## To Silvia

Silvia, rememberest thou
Yet that sweet time of thine abode on earth,
When beauty graced thy brow
And fired thine eyes, so radiant and so gay;
And thou, so joyous, yet of pensive mood,
Didst pass on youth's fair way?

        The chambers calm and still,
The sunny paths around,
Did to thy song resound,
When thou, upon thy handiwork intent,
Wast seated, full of joy
At the fair future where thy hopes were bound.
It was the fragrant month of flowery May,
And thus went by thy day.

        I leaving oft behind
The labours and the vigils of my mind,
That did my life consume,
And of my being far the best entomb,
Bade from the casement of my father's house
Mine ears give heed unto thy silver song,
And to thy rapid hand
That swept with skill the spinning thread along.
I watched the sky serene,
The radiant ways and flowers,
And here the sea, the mountain there, expand.
No mortal tongue can tell
What made my bosom swell.

What thoughts divinely sweet,
What hopes, O Silvia! and what souls were ours!
In what guise did we meet
Our destiny and life?
When I remember such aspiring flown,
Fierce pain invades my soul,
Which nothing can console,
And my misfortune I again bemoan.
O Nature, void of ruth,
Why not give some return
For those fair promises? Why full of fraud
Thy wretched offspring spurn?

Thou ere the herbs by winter were destroyed,
Led to the grave by an unknown disease,
Didst perish, tender blossom: thy life's flower
Was not by thee enjoyed;
Nor heard, thy heart to please,
The admiration of thy raven hair
Or of the enamoured glances of thine eyes;
Nor thy companions in the festive hour
Spoke of love's joys and sighs.

Ere long my hope as well
Was dead and gone. By cruel Fate's decree
Was youthfulness denied
Unto my years. Ah me!
How art thou past for aye,
Thou dear companion of my earlier day,
My hope so much bewailed!
Is this the world? Are these
The joys, the loves, the labours and the deeds
Whereof so often we together spoke?
Is this the doom to which mankind proceeds?

When truth before thee lay
Revealed, thou sankest; and thy dying hand
Pointed to death, a figure of cold gloom,
And to a distant tomb.

—*translated from the Italian by Francis Henry Cliffe*

# SENSUAL LOVE

## Algernon Charles Swinburne

Love and Sleep

Lying asleep between the strokes of night
   I saw my love lean over my sad bed,
   Pale as the duskiest lily's leaf or head,
Smooth-skinned and dark, with bare throat made to bite,
Too wan for blushing and too warm for white,
   But perfect-coloured without white or red.
   And her lips opened amorously, and said—
I wist not what, saving one word—Delight.

And all her face was honey to my mouth,
   And all her body pasture to mine eyes;
     The long lithe arms and hotter hands than fire,
The quivering flanks, hair smelling of the south,
     The bright light feet, the splendid supple thighs
     And glittering eyelids of my soul's desire.

# Ovid

## Elegy 5

In summer's heat and mid-time of the day,
To rest my limbs upon a bed I lay,
One window shut, the other open stood,
Which gave such light as twinkles in a wood
Like twilight glimpse at setting of the sun,
Or night being past and yet not day begun.
Such light to shamefaced maidens must be shown,
Where they may sport, and seem to be unknown.
Then came Corinna in a long, loose gown,
Her white neck hid with tresses hanging down,
Resembling fair Semiramis going to bed,
Or Lais of a thousand wooers sped.
I snatched her gown, being thin the harm was small,
Yet strived she to be covered therewithal,
And, striving thus as one that would be chaste,
Betrayed herself, and yielded at the last.
Stark naked as she stood before mine eye,
Not one wen in her body could I spy.
What arms and shoulders did I touch and see?
How apt her breasts were to be pressed by me?
How smooth a belly under her waist saw I?
How large a leg, and what a lusty thigh?
To leave the rest, all liked me passing well;
I clinged her naked body, down she fell.
Judge you the rest. Being tired, she bade me kiss.
Jove send me more such afternoons as this.

— *translated from the Latin by Christopher Marlowe*

# Robert Herrick

To the Virgins, to Make Much of Time


Gather ye rosebuds while ye may,
    Old Time is still a-flying:
And this same flower that smiles today
    Tomorrow will be dying.

The glorious lamp of heaven, the sun,
    The higher he's a-getting,
The sooner will his race be run,
    And nearer he's to setting.

That age is best which is the first,
    When youth and blood are warmer;
But being spent, the worse, and worst
    Times still succeed the former.

Then be not coy, but use your time,
    And while ye may, go marry:
For having lost but once your prime,
    You may for ever tarry.

# Petronius Arbiter

## Doing

Doing, a filthy pleasure is, and short;
And done, we straight repent us of the sport:
Let us not rush blindly on unto it,
Like lustful beasts, that only know to do it:
For lust will languish, and that heat decay,
But thus, thus, keeping endless holiday,
Let us together closely lie and kiss,
There is no labour, nor no shame in this;
This hath pleased, doth please, and long will please; never
Can this decay, but is beginning ever.

*—translated from the Latin by Ben Jonson*

# Sara Teasdale

## The Kiss

Before you kissed me only winds of heaven
Had kissed me, and the tenderness of rain—
Now you have come, how can I care for kisses
Like theirs again?

I sought the sea, she sent her winds to meet me,
They surged about me singing of the south—
I turned my head away to keep still holy
Your kiss upon my mouth.

And swift sweet rains of shining April weather
Found not my lips where living kisses are;
I bowed my head lest they put out my glory
As rain puts out a star.

I am my love's and he is mine forever,
Sealed with a seal and safe forevermore—
Think you that I could let a beggar enter
Where a king stood before?

# Andrei Voznesensky

## Dead Still

Now, with your palms on the blades of my shoulders,
Let us embrace:
Let there be only your lips' breath on my face,
Only, behind our backs, the plunge of rollers.

Our backs, which like two shells in moonlight shine,
Are shut behind us now;
We lie here huddled, listening brow to brow,
Like life's twin formula or double sign.

In folly's world-wide wind
Our shoulders shield from the weather
The calm we now beget together,
Like a flame held between hand and hand.

Does each cell have a soul within it?
If so, fling open all your little doors,
And all your souls shall flutter like the linnet
In the cages of my pores.

Nothing is hidden that shall not be known.
Yet by no storm of scorn shall we
Be pried from this embrace, and left alone
Like muted shells forgetful of the sea.

Meanwhile, O load of stress and bother,
Lie on the shells of our backs in a great heap:
It will press us closer, one to the other.

We are asleep.
*—translated from the Russian by Richard Wilbur*

# Claude McKay

## A Red Flower

Your lips are like a southern lily red,
Wet with soft rain-kisses of the night,
In which the brown bee buries deep its head,
When still the dawn's a silver sea of light.
Your lips betray the secret of your soul,
The dark delicious essence that is you,
A mystery of life, the flaming goal
I seek through mazy pathways strange and new.
Your lips are the red symbol of a dream.
What visions of warm lilies they impart,
That line the green bank of a fair blue stream,
With butterflies and bees close to each heart!
Brown bees that murmur sounds of music rare,
That softly fall upon the languorous breeze,
Wafting them gently on the quiet air
Among untended avenues of trees.
O were I hovering, a bee, to probe
Deep down within your scented heart, fair flower,
Enfolded by your soft vermilion robe,
Amorous of sweets, for but one perfect hour!

# Sappho

## Desire

Desire shakes me once again,
here is that melting of my limbs.
It is a creeping thing, and bittersweet.
I can do nothing to resist.

*—translated from the Greek by Suzy Q. Groden*


# Robert Browning

## Life in a Love

Escape me?
Never—
Beloved!
While I am I, and you are you,
    So long as the world contains us both,
    Me the loving and you the loth,
While the one eludes, must the other pursue.
My life is a fault at last, I fear:
It seems too much like a fate, indeed!
Though I do my best I shall scarce succeed.
But what if I fail of my purpose here?
It is but to keep the nerves at strain,
To dry one's eyes and laugh at a fall,
And, baffled, get up and begin again,—
So the chase takes up one's life, that's all.

While, look but once from your farthest bound
At me so deep in the dust and dark,
No sooner the old hope goes to ground
Than a new one, straight to the self-same mark,
I shape me—
Ever
Removed!


## Meleager

### On the Lake of Love


Asklepias adores making love. She gazes at a man,
her aquamarine eyes calm like the summer seas,
and persuades him to go boating on the lake of love.

*—translated from the Greek by Willis Barnstone*

# James Whitcomb Riley

## Her Beautiful Hands

O your hands—they are strangely fair!
Fair—for the jewels that sparkle there,—
Fair—for the witchery of the spell
That ivory keys alone can tell;
But when their delicate touches rest
Here in my own do I love them best,
As I clasp with eager, acquisitive spans
My glorious treasure of beautiful hands!

Marvelous—wonderful—beautiful hands!
They can coax roses to bloom in the strands
Of your brown tresses; and ribbons will twine,
Under mysterious touches of thine,
Into such knots as entangle the soul
And fetter the heart under such a control
As only the strength of my love understands—
My passionate love for your beautiful hands.

As I remember the first fair touch
Of those beautiful hands that I love so much,
I seem to thrill as I then was thrilled,
Kissing the glove that I found unfilled—
When I met your gaze, and the queenly bow,
As you said to me, laughingly, 'Keep it now!'…
And dazed and alone in a dream I stand,
Kissing this ghost of your beautiful hand.

When first I loved, in the long ago,
And held your hand as I told you so—
Pressed and caressed it and gave it a kiss

And said 'I could die for a hand like this!'
Little I dreamed love's fullness yet
Had to ripen when eyes were wet
And prayers were vain in their wild demands
For one warm touch of your beautiful hands.

Beautiful Hands!—O Beautiful Hands!
Could you reach out of the alien lands
Where you are lingering, and give me, to-night
Only a touch—were it ever so light—
My heart were soothed, and my weary brain
Would lull itself into rest again;
For there is no solace the world commands
Like the caress of your beautiful hands.

# Anonymous

## Request

Give me yourself one hour; I do not crave
    For any love, or even thought, of me.
Come, as a Sultan may caress a slave
    And then forget for ever, utterly.

Come! as west winds, that passing, cool and wet,
    O'er desert places, leave them fields in flower;
And all my life, for I shall not forget,
    Will keep the fragrance of that perfect hour!

        *—translated from the Sanksrit by Laurence Hope*

# Gaius Valerius Catullus

### My Sweetest Lesbia

My sweetest Lesbia, let us live and love,
And though the sager sort our deeds reprove,
Let us not weigh them. Heaven's great lamps do dive
Into their west, and straight again revive,
But soon as once set is our little light,
Then must we sleep one ever-during night.

If all would lead their lives in love like me,
Then bloody swords and armor should not be;
No drum nor trumpet peaceful sleeps should move,
Unless alarm came from the camp of love.
But fools do live, and waste their little light,
And seek with pain their ever-during night.

When timely death my life and fortune ends,
Let not my hearse be vexed with mourning friends,
But let all lovers, rich in triumph, come
And with sweet pastimes grace my happy tomb;
And Lesbia, close up thou my little light,
And crown with love my ever-during night.

# Imra'u'l-Kais

*from* The Mu'allakát


Love that wellnigh had ceased from welling,
Love rose high in my heart again
For Sulaimà, down in 'Arar dwelling,
When Taimar's rills were alive with rain.
Oh, I see thee, Kinána's daughter,
And the howdahs in the mist of dawn
Gliding by, like ships on water—
They passed and thou wert gone!—
Like tall palms undeflowered,
For the sword of their clan is drawn
Until their maiden
Boughs be laden
With ripe yellow bunches and lowered,
A wonder to look upon!
Proudly the sons of Rabdá ride
At harvest-tide.

But the women those howdahs nestled,
More fair seemed they
Than statues, on marble chiselled,
Of Sukf, in the valley where Sájúm
Foams to the Persian bay.
Safely fended,
Softly tended,
With pearls and rubies and beads of gold
And gums of delicate odour in pyxes old,
Spicy musk and aloes and myrrh—
Sweet, oh, sweet is the breath of her
Who stole from thee, Sulaimà, my love away.

The cord is cut asunder that tied me so true of yore,
When darting a covert eye to thy tent close-veiled
I saw thee and paled
And trembled at the sight,
As one trembles who overnight
Drank deep, and in the morning his cup is filled once more.

*—translated from the Arabic by Reynold A. Nicholson*

## William Butler Yeats

### Leda and the Swan

A sudden blow: the great wings beating still
Above the staggering girl, her thighs caressed
By the dark webs, her nape caught in his bill,
He holds her helpless breast upon his breast.

How can those terrified vague fingers push
The feathered glory from her loosening thighs?
And how can body, laid in that white rush,
But feel the strange heart beating where it lies?

A shudder in the loins engenders there
The broken wall, the burning roof and tower
And Agamemnon dead.
                              Being so caught up,
So mastered by the brute blood of the air,
Did she put on his knowledge with his power
Before the indifferent beak could let her drop?

# Asclepiades

To a Coy Maiden

Believe me love, it is not good
To hoard a mortal maidenhood;
In Hades thou wilt never find,
Maiden, a lover to thy mind;
Love's for the living! presently
Ashes and dust in death are we!

*—translated from the Greek by Andrew Lang*

# Arthur Symons

Leves Amores

Your kisses, and the way you curl,
Delicious and distracting girl,
Into one's arms, and round about,
Inextricably in and out,
Twining luxuriously, as twine
The clasping tangles of the vine;
So loving to be loved, so gay
And greedy for our holiday;
Strong to embrace and long to kiss,
And strenuous for the sharper bliss,
A little tossing sea of sighs,
Till the slow calm seal up your eyes.
And then how prettily you sleep!
You nestle close and let me keep
My straying fingers in the nest
Of your warm comfortable breast;
And as I dream, lying awake,
Of sleep well wasted for your sake,
I feel the very pulse and heat
Of your young life-blood beat, and beat
With mine; and you are mine; my sweet!

# Theocritus

*from* Seduction

Thus did this happy pair their love dispense
With mutual joys, and gratified their sense;
The God of Love was there a bidden guest;
And present at his own mysterious Feast.
His azure mantle underneath he spread,
And scattered roses on the nuptial bed;
While folded in each other's arms they lay,
He blew the flames, and furnished out the play,
And from their foreheads wiped the balmy sweat away.
First rose the maid, and with a glowing face
Her downcast eyes beheld her print upon the grass;
Thence to her herd she sped herself in haste:
The bridegroom started from his trance at last,
And piping homeward jocundly he passed.

*—translated from the Greek by John Dryden*

# William Cartwright

## No Platonic Love

Tell me no more of minds embracing minds,
    And hearts exchang'd for hearts;
That spirits spirits meet, as winds do winds,
    And mix their subt'lest parts;
That two unbodied essences may kiss,
And then like Angels, twist and feel one Bliss.

I was that silly thing that once was wrought
    To practise this thin love;
I climb'd from sex to soul, from soul to thought;
    But thinking there to move,
Headlong I rolled from thought to soul, and then
From soul I lighted at the sex again.

As some strict down-looked men pretend to fast,
    Who yet in closets eat;
So lovers who profess they spirits taste,
    Feed yet on grosser meat;
I know they boast they souls to souls convey,
Howe'r they meet, the body is the way.

Come, I will undeceive thee, they that tread
    Those vain aerial ways,
Are like young heirs and alchemists misled
    To waste their wealth and days,
For searching thus to be for ever rich,
They only find a med'cine for the itch.

# Gaius Valerius Catullus

Come and let us live my Dear,
Let us love and never fear,
What the sourest Fathers say:
Brightest *Sol* that dies today
Lives again as blithe tomorrow,
But if we dark sons of sorrow
Set; o then, how long a Night
Shuts the Eyes of our short light!
Then let amorous kisses dwell
On our lips, begin to tell
A Thousand, and a Hundred, score
An Hundred, and a Thousand more,
Till another Thousand smother
That, and that wipe off another.
Thus at last when we have numb'red
Many a Thousand, many a Hundred;
We'll confound the reckoning quite,
And lose ourselves in wild delight:
While our joys so multiply,
As shall mock the envious eye.

—*translated from the Latin by Richard Crashaw*

# Thomas Moore

## Did Not

'Twas a new feeling—something more
Than we had dared to own before,
     Which then we hid not;
We saw it in each other's eye,
And wished, in every half-breathed sigh,
     To speak, but did not.

She felt my lips' impassioned touch—
'Twas the first time I dared so much,
     And yet she chid not;
But whispered o'er my burning brow,
'Oh! do you doubt I love you now?'
     Sweet soul! I did not.

Warmly I felt her bosom thrill,
I pressed it closer, closer still,
     Though gently bid not;
Till—oh! the world hath seldom heard
Of lovers, who so nearly erred,
     And yet, who did not.

# Andrew Marvell

## To His Coy Mistress

    Had we but world enough, and time,
This coyness, lady, were no crime.
We would sit down, and think which way
To walk, and pass our long loves day.
Thou by the Indian Ganges' side
Shouldst rubies find; I by the tide
Of Humber would complain. I would
Love you ten years before the flood,
And you should, if you please, refuse
Till the conversion of the Jews.
My vegetable love should grow
Vaster than empires and more slow;
An hundred years should go to praise
Thine eyes, and on thy forehead gaze;
Two hundred to adore each breast,
But thirty thousand to the rest;
An age at least to every part,
And the last age should show your heart.
For, lady, you deserve this state,
Nor would I love at lower rate.

    But at my back I always hear
Time's wingéd chariot hurrying near;
And yonder all before us lie
Deserts of vast eternity.
Thy beauty shall no more be found.
Nor, in thy marble vault, shall sound
My echoing song; then worms shall try
That long-preserved virginity,
And your quaint honor turn to dust,

And into ashes all my lust:
The grave's a fine and private place,
But none, I think, do there embrace.

   Now therefore, while the youthful hue
Sits on thy skin like morning dew,
And while thy willing soul transpires
At every pore with instant fires,
Now let us sport us while we may,
And now, like amorous birds of prey,
Rather at once our time devour
Than languish in his slow-chapped power.
Let us roll all our strength and all
Our sweetness up into one ball,
And tear our pleasures with rough strife
Thorough the iron gates of life:
Thus, though we cannot make our sun
Stand still, yet we will make him run.

# Robert Herrick

## The Night Piece: To Julia

Her eyes the glow-worm lend thee,
The shooting stars attend thee;
   And the elves also,
   Whose little eyes glow
Like the sparks of fire, befriend thee.

No will-o'-the-wisp mislight thee,
Nor snake or slow-worm bite thee;
   But on, on thy way
   Not making a stay,
Since ghost there's none to affright thee.

Let not the dark thee cumber:
What though the moon does slumber?
   The stars of the night
   Will lend thee their light
Like tapers clear without number.

Then, Julia, let me woo thee,
Thus, thus to come unto me;
   And when I shall meet
   Thy silv'ry feet
My soul I'll pour into thee.

# SPIRITUAL LOVE

## Percy Bysshe Shelley

One Word is Too Often Profaned

One word is too often profaned
    For me to profane it;
One feeling too falsely disdained
    For thee to disdain it;
One hope is too like despair
    For prudence to smother;
And pity from thee more dear
    Than that from another.
I can give not what men call love;
    But wilt thou accept not
The worship the heart lifts above
    And the heavens reject not,—
The desire of the moth for the star,
    Of the night for the morrow,
The devotion to something afar
    From the sphere of our sorrow?

# Rábi'a of Basra

Two ways I love Thee: selfishly,
And next, as worthy is of Thee.
'Tis selfish love that I do naught
Save think on Thee with every thought.
'Tis purest love when Thou dost raise
The veil to my adoring gaze.
Not mine the praise in that or this:
Thine is the praise in both, I wis.

—*translated from the Arabic by Reynold A. Nicholson*

# Leigh Hunt

## Abou Ben Adhem

Abou Ben Adhem (may his tribe increase!)
Awoke one night from a deep dream of peace,
And saw, within the moonlight in his room,
Making it rich, and like a lily in bloom,
An Angel writing in a book of gold:—
Exceeding peace had made Ben Adhem bold,
And to the Presence in the room he said,
'What writest thou?'—The Vision raised its head,
And with a look made of all sweet accord
Answered, 'The names of those who love the Lord.'
'And is mine one?' said Abou. 'Nay, not so,'
Replied the Angel. Abou spoke more low,
But cheerily still, and said, 'I pray thee, then,
Write me as one that loves his fellow men.'

The Angel wrote and vanished. The next night
It came again with a great wakening light,
And showed the names whom love of God had blessed,
And, lo! Ben Adhem's name led all the rest.

# San Juan de la Cruz

## The Dark Night

One dark night,
Fired with love's urgent longings
Ah, the sheer grace!
I went out unseen,
My house being now all stilled;

In darkness, and secure,
But the secret ladder, disguised,
Ah, the sheer grace!
In darkness and concealment,
My house being now all stilled;

On that glad night,
In secret, for no one saw me,
Nor did I look at anything,
With no other light or guide

Than the one that burned in my heart;
This guided me
More surely than the light of noon
To where He waited for me
Him I knew so well
In a place where no one else appeared.

O guiding night!
O night more lovely than the dawn!
O night that has united
The Lover with His beloved,
Transforming the beloved in her Lover.

Upon my flowering breast
Which I kept wholly for Him alone,
There He lay sleeping,
And I caressing Him
There in a breeze from the fanning cedars.

When the breeze blew from the turret
Parting His hair,
He wounded my neck
With his gentle hand,
Suspending all my senses.
I abandoned and forgot myself,
Laying my face on my Beloved;
All things ceased; I went out from myself,
Leaving my cares
Forgotten among the lilies.

*—translated from the Spanish by Kieran Kavanaugh*
*and Otilio Rodriguez*

# Edwin Markham

## Outwitted

He drew a circle that shut me out—
    Heretic, rebel, a thing to flout.
But love and I had the wit to win:
    We drew a circle that took him in!


# Jalálu'ddín Rúmí

*from* Díwán-i Shams-i Tabríz

If there be any lover in the world, O Moslems, 'tis I.
If there be any believer, infidel, or Christian hermit, 'tis I.
The wine-dregs, the cupbearer, the minstrel, the harp and the music,
The beloved, the candle, the drink and the joy of the drunken—'tis I.
The two-and-seventy creeds and sects in the world
Do not really exist: I swear by God that every creed and sect—'tis I.
Earth and air and water and fire—knowest thou what they are?
Earth and air and water and fire, nay, body and soul too—'tis I.
Truth and falsehood, good and evil, ease and difficulty from first to last,
Knowledge and learning and asceticism and piety and faith—'tis I.
The fire of Hell, be assured, with its flaming limbos,
Yes, and Paradise and Eden and the houris—'tis I.
This earth and heaven with all that they hold,
Angels, peris, genies, and mankind—'tis I.

*—translated from the Persian by Reynold A. Nicholson*

# George Herbert

*from* Divinitie

*Love God, and love your neighbour. Watch and pray.*
    *Do as ye would be done unto.*
O dark instructions; ev'n as dark as day!
    Who can these Gordian knots undo?

# Solomon Ibn Gabirol

## The Love of God

To Thee, O living God, my being yearns,
For Thee my soul consumes, my spirit burns.

Within Thy chosen people's hearts Thy glory
Inhabits, be they babes or fathers hoary,

To bind Thy chosen to Thy chariot wheels.
And with the radiance that Thee conceals

I fill my heart and make for my delight
A lampstand set beside me in the night.

The wisest weary them to comprehend
Thy mystery, then how should I ascend

The secret of Thy glorious shrine to tell?
Thy shining semblance is unsearchable.

Then let my craving to my own soul turn
To find the wealth divine for which I yearn.

For Wisdom's house is as of sapphires builded,
Her pavement as with gold of Ophir gilded.

Within the body is her hidden lair,
Like a young lion she is couchant there.

She is my bliss and joy in lamentation,
She is my thinking cap of meditation.

What man dare all her beauty's praises sum,
Or be to her perfections wholly dumb?

Answer her swiftly, God of grace above,
For she is sick with longing for Thy love.

'Gently, dear damsel, sip salvation's water,
For thou, most dazzling maiden, art My daughter.'

*—translated from the Hebrew by Israel Zangwill*
*for the Jewish Publication Society of America*

# Richard Crashaw

*from* A Hymn to the Name and Honour of the
Admirable Saint Teresa


Love, thou are absolute, sole Lord
Of life and death. To prove the word,
We'll now appeal to none of all
Those thy old soldiers, great and tall,
Ripe men of martyrdom, that could reach down
With strong arms their triumphant crown:
Such as could with lusty breath
Speak loud, unto the face of death,
Their great Lord's glorious name; to none
Of those whose spacious bosoms spread a throne
For love at large to fill. Spare blood and sweat:
We'll see Him take a private seat,
And make His mansion in the mild
And milky soul of a soft child.

# Ibnu'l-Fárid

*from* The Díwán

With my Beloved I alone have been
When secrets tenderer than evening airs
Passed, and the Vision blest
Was granted to my prayers,
That crowned me, else obscure, with endless fame,
The while amazed between
His beauty and His majesty
I stood in silent ecstasy,
Revealing that which o'er my spirit went and came.
Lo, in His face commingled
Is every charm and grace;
The whole of Beauty singled
Into a perfect face
Beholding Him would cry,
'There is no god but He, and He is the Most High!'

*—translated from the Arabic by Reynold A. Nicholson*


# Robert Browning

*from* Easter Day

Upon the ground
'That in the story had been found
Too much love! How could God love *so*?'
He who in all His works below
Adapted to the needs of man,
Made love the basis of the plan,—
*Did* love, as was demonstrated.

165

# Anonymous

## Hymn to the Virgin

Thou Flower of flowers! I'll follow thee,
And sing thy praise unweariedly:
Best of the best! O, may I ne'er
From thy pure service flee!

Lady, to thee I turn my eyes,
On thee my trusting hope relies;
O, let thy spirit, smiling here,
Chase my anxieties!

Most Holy Virgin! Tired and faint,
I pour my melancholy plaint;
Yet lift a tremulous thought to thee,
Alas, 'midst mortal taint.

Thou Ocean-Star! Thou Port of joy!
From pain, and sadness, and annoy,
O, rescue me, O, comfort me,
Bright Lady of the Sky!

Thy mercy is a boundless mine;
Freedom from care, and life are thine;
He recks not, faints not, fears not, who
Trusts in thy power divine.

Unjustly I do suffer wrong,
Despair and darkness guide my song;
I see no other, come do thou
Waft my weak bark along!

*—translated from the Spanish by Henry W. Longfellow*

## Samuel Taylor Coleridge

*from* The Rime of the Ancient Mariner

He prayeth best, who loveth best
    All things both great and small;
For the dear God who loveth us,
    He made and loveth all.


## Friedrich von Schiller

Three Words of Strength

There are three lessons I would write,
Three words, as with a burning pen,
In tracings of eternal light,
Upon the hearts of men.

Have Hope. Though clouds environ round,
And gladness hides her face in scorn,
Put off the shadow from thy brow:
No night but hath its morn.

Have Faith. Where'er thy bark is driven—
The calm's disport, the tempest's mirth—
Know this: God rules the host of heaven,
The inhabitants of earth.

Have love. Not love alone for one,
But man, as man thy brother call;
And scatter, like a circling sun,
Thy charities on all.

*—from the German, translator unknown*

167

# Kahlil Gibran

*from* Dam'ah wa Ibtisamah

You are my brother and I love you;
I love you
at prayer in your mosque,
at your worship in your synagogue,
at your devotions in your church;
for you and I are the sons of one religion—
the spirit.

*—translated from the Arabic by Suheil Bushrui*

# Henry Wadsworth Longfellow

The Arrow and the Song

I shot an arrow into the air,
It fell to earth, I knew not where;
For, so swiftly it flew, the sight
Could not follow it in its flight.

I breathed a song into the air,
It fell to earth, I knew not where;
For who has sight so keen and strong
That it can follow the flight of song?

Long, long afterward, in an oak
I found the arrow, still unbroke;
And the song, from beginning to end,
I found again in the heart of a friend.

# Ibnu'l-'Arabí

*from* Tarjumán al-Ashwáq

My heart is capable of every form:
A cloister for the monk, a fane for idols,
A pasture for gazelles, the votary's Kaaba,
The tables of the Torah, the Koran.
Love is the faith I hold: wherever turn
His camels, still the one true faith is mine.

—*translated from the Arabic by Reynold A. Nicholson*

# George Herbert

## Love

Love bade me welcome; yet my soul drew back,
    Guilty of dust and sin.
But quick-ey'd Love, observing me grow slack
    From my first entrance in,
Drew nearer to me, sweetly questioning
    If I lack'd anything.

'A guest,' I answer'd, 'worthy to be here';
    Love said, 'You shall be he.'
'I, the unkind, ungrateful? Ah, my dear,
    I cannot look on Thee.'
Love took my hand and smiling did reply,
    'Who made the eyes but I?'

'Truth, Lord; but I have marr'd them; let my shame
    Go where it doth deserve.'
'And know you not,' says Love, 'who bore the blame?'
    'My dear, then I will serve.'
'You must sit down,' says Love, 'and taste My meat.'
    So I did sit and eat.

# Halláj

*from* Díwán al-Halláj

Betwixt me and Thee there lingers as 'it is I' that torments me.
Ah, of Thy grace, take away this 'I' from between us!

I am He whom I love, and He whom I love is I,
We are two spirits dwelling in one body.
If thou seest me, thou seest Him,
And if thou seest Him, thou seest us both.

*—translated from the Arabic by Reynold A. Nicholson*

## Anonymous

Love Song

Why is it that we cannot be together? It causes me grief.
If it is never to be here on earth, in the blue heavens beyond it will
work out for us.
[God] take pity on me. I am grieving.

*—translated from the Lakota (Native American)
by Kevin Locke*

# Acknowledgements

In the preparation of this volume, I have received much valuable help and guidance from Ms Juliet Mabey, the poet Francis Warner, and Professor Miles L. Bradbury.

Acknowledgement is hereby extended to the following for permission to publish copyright material:

Alfred A. Knopf, Inc., a division of Random House, Inc., for permission to publish passages by Kahlil Gibran from *The Prophet*.

Alida Gubag for her translation of the anonymous Karkar Island Love Song.

A.P. Watt Limited on behalf of Gráinne Yeats for permission to publish 'Leda and the Swan' and 'The Lover Tells of the Rose in his Heart'.

Brian Read for permission to publish 'Leves Amores' by Arthur Symons.

David Higham Associates Limited for permission to publish a passage by Dame Edith Sitwell from *Heart and Mind*.

Edward Lucie-Smith for permission to publish his translation of Alain Chartier.

The Estate of Kathleen Raine for permission to publish 'Amo Ergo Sum' by Kathleen Raine.

Francis Warner for permission to publish 'Lyric'.

Harold Wright for permission to publish his translations of two anonymous Japanese poems, and poems by Lady Nakatomi, Lady Kasa, and Lord Asukabe.

Hilary M. Freeman for permission to publish a passage from *Days of Creation*.

The Johns Hopkins University for permission to publish Eleanor L. Turnbull's translation of Juan Ramón Jiménez's poem, 'Were I Reborn'. Eleanor Turnbull Papers, MS 55, Special Collections, Sheridan Libraries, The Johns Hopkins University.

Kevin Locke for permission to publish his translation of two anonymous Lakota 'Love Songs'.

The Markham Archives at Horrmann Library, Wagner College for permission to publish 'Outwitted' by Edwin Markham.

# Index of first lines

# Index of authors